DESERT GARDENING

By the Editors of Sunset Magazine and Sunset Books

Lane Publishing Co. · Menlo Park, California

FOREWORD

We owe this book to the many desert gardeners who realize that every plant they see in the gardens around them, except for the natives, was brought into the desert on a trial-and-error basis—or at best as a calculated risk—and who, with a free-wheeling experimental spirit, are carrying on new trials.

We owe this book to the progressive nurserymen, university researchers, county agents, horticulturists, botanists, and landscape architects whose knowledge and experience have for years been chronicled in the garden pages of *Sunset Magazine's* Desert Edition.

And so we dedicate this book to our garden-minded friends who will make it necessary to revise this first edition at some future date—revise it to include their newly found experiences and their ever-expanding lists of plants proved to be adapted to their desert.

Editor, Sunset Books: David E. Clark

Thirteenth printing April 1983

CONTENTS

ON THE COVER: A Tucson garden features prickly pear cactus and colorful petunias. Native palo verde trees grow behind the house. Photo by Richard Jepperson.

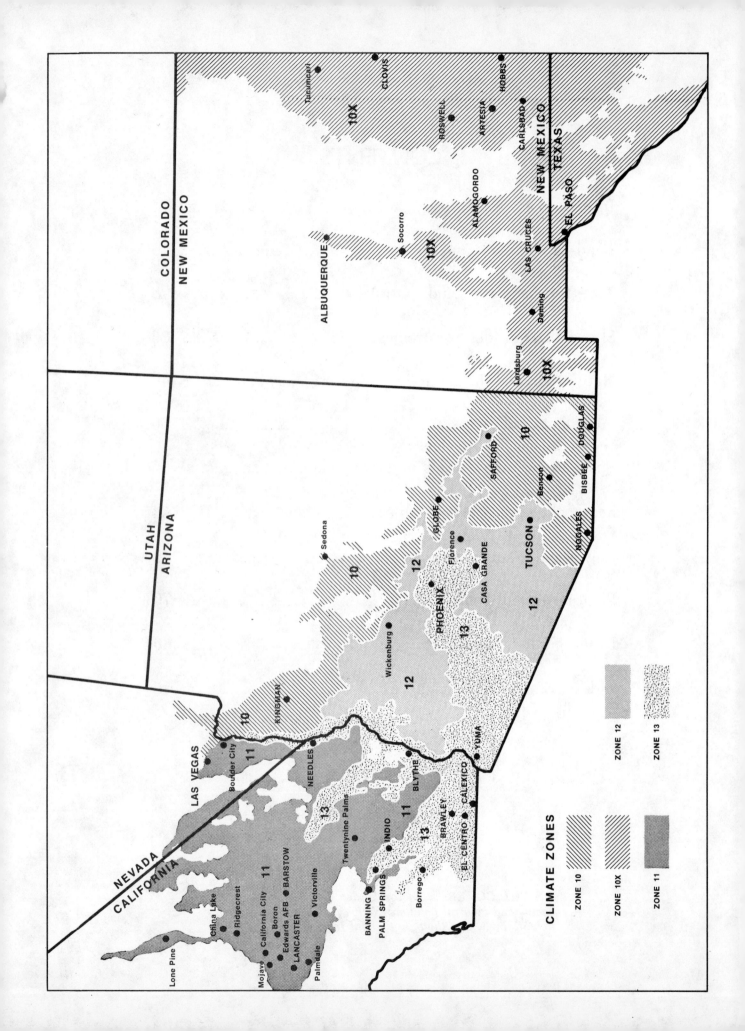

INTRODUCTION: WHAT IS DIFFERENT ABOUT GARDENING IN THE DESERT?

Wherever the desert gardener finds himself—in southern Nevada or California, in Arizona, New Mexico, or Texas—he is working with a very special mixture of soil, water, sunlight, air, cold and heat that offers challenges and unusual opportunities.

The challenges are often dramatic and therefore are most frequently talked about. The desert is hot. The desert is windy. The desert is dry. True. It is all these things and more. In every desert there are days and months just right for good growing—and good living. In some deserts, spring comes in October and lasts until June.

Gardeners meet the challenge of the desert in different ways. Some join with the desert in their gardening; some hold it back and create their own oasis; some like part oasis and part desert.

To the newcomer to the desert, blessed (or cursed) with an adventurous spirit, gardening is full of surprises, frustrations, and exciting rewards. The newcomer is not burdened by the memory of the record-breaking cold winter; his failures are yet to come. He blithely goes ahead and plants what shouldn't be planted, and now and then he gets away with it. Thus the kinds and variety of plants that will grow in each desert is increased year by year.

The desert gardener plays a more powerful role than gardeners generally. He can dramatically change the climate in and around his house. By his plantings he can tame the wind and the sun, cool the house walls with shade and green growth, carpet the soil with cool green.

Perhaps the greatest reward of gardening in the desert is the exuberant response in growth of plants when you have done right by them. Give a little wind protection and, presto, a different plant. Keep watering evergreens through the winter months and they are the tallest in town. Give a tree in a lawn a deep, slow soaking once a month with an extra application of fertilizer over the grass and marvel at its growth.

If this book encourages you to experiment with plants and helps you do right by the plants in your garden, it will have served a good purpose.

What deserts are we talking about?

In this book we are talking about gardening in five different desert climates:

Arizona's High Desert (10)
High Desert of New Mexico and Texas (10X)
California's Medium to High Desert (11)
Arizona's Intermediate Desert (12)
Low Desert of California and Arizona (13)

In talking about plants "adapted to the desert", it is often necessary to designate *which* desert. A number does the job faster than a descriptive phrase. To avoid confusion on the part of users of this and the *Sunset Western Garden Book*, we recognize the same groups of desert climates and use the same climate zone numbers as does the *Western Garden Book*. Because a general book on desert gardening wouldn't be complete without it, an additional climate zone has been added—High Desert of New Mexico and Texas (10X).

ZONE 10 Arizona's High Desert

Here we are looking at the climates of Bisbee, Benson, Globe, Douglas, Kingman, Sedona.

This is the high desert. Elevations range from 3,300 to 5,000 feet. It has a more definite winter season than Arizona's intermediate desert. The number of nights below 32° is greater, and night temperatures drop below 28° more frequently. However these winters are a series of frosts rather than freezes. Mean daytime temperatures in December, January, and February are from 55° to 60°.

The lowest temperatures recorded range from 6° to 10°; lowest in ten years 9° to 16°.

That these are relatively mild winters can be seen in frequent and successful planting of such tender evergreens as star jasmine and xylosma.

Summer temperatures are mild as desert temperatures go. The number of days with temperatures of 90° and above range from 100 to 150. But the mean maximum temperatures in July and August are *below* 100°. So, while winter cold limits the number of subtropicals that can be grown, other features of

Map at left shows five Southwest desert zones. Keep your climate zone in mind when going down lists of shrubs, other basic landscape plants in this book.

Pool, shade trees, and green lawn—desirable in any desert garden. (See p. 19.)

this climate are most favorable to an extremely wide variety of plants.

Summers are hot enough to grow the shrubs and trees that need a good quantity of heat, such as olives, pomegranate, and crape myrtle.

Summers are mild enough to allow the full quota of annuals and perennials to flourish through the summer.

Winters are cold enough to give the winter chilling needed by deciduous fruits, flowering shrubs, and cold climate perennials.

This climate has the additional advantage of more rainfall than the other deserts. For example, the annual rainfall of Globe ranges from 15 to 22 inches; Benson, 10 to 15 inches; Douglas, 12 to 15 inches; Kingman, 10 to 15 inches; Sedona, 16 to 23 inches. Half of the annual rainfall occurs in July and August.

Plants in this high desert are not subjected to the stresses of wind to the degree they are in the high deserts of California.

To illustrate the wide variety of plants that can be grown in this climate, here is a partial inventory of plants in one garden in Sedona: castor bean, Utah juniper, fountain grass (*Pennisetum setaceum*), snow-on-the-mountain, mondo grass, pampas grass, snow-in-summer, nicotiana, festuca, roses, purple-leaf plum, dahlias, petunias, phlox, yucca, loquat, flowering quince, euonymus, fatsia, daylilies, Apache plume, pinon pine, forsythia, vinca, dusty miller, and camellias.

ZONE 10 X   High Desert of New Mexico and Texas

This climate carries us one step beyond the desert climates included in the *Sunset Western Garden Book*, but not too far beyond. It is the climate of the cities in the chart below and their environs.

Gardening in this portion of the Southwest has much in common with gardening in the high deserts of Arizona. The soil and water management problems are similar. In both areas gardeners know something about desert winds. The significant difference is in the lower winter temperatures.

From the plant's viewpoint there are two climates within this climate: mild-winter climate represented by El Paso, and the relatively cold-winter climate represented by Albuquerque.

Some of the plants that are freely used in El Paso are risky or need special attention in Albuquerque. The few examples below illustrate the differences. In Albuquerque you find:

Crape myrtle. Best on south wall in protected patio.

India hawthorn (*Raphiolepis indica*).   Not hardy; however, the round-leafed *R. umbellata* (formerly *R. ovata*) is hardy.

Pines. The Aleppo pine, favorite in all the mild-winter desert areas, is not for this climate; the

---

SOME CITIES IN ZONE 10X

	Elevation	Annual rainfall	Record low	Nights below 32°	Days above 90°
EL PASO, TEXAS	3920'	7.89"	—6°	55	107
LORDSBURG, N. M.	4245'	10.10"	2°	96	124
ALAMOGORDO	4320'	9.8"	—8°	89	113
DEMING	4331'	8.9"	—7°	100	111
ROSWELL	3610'	11.6"	—8°	107	111
ALBUQUERQUE	5200'	8.0"	—10°	105	75

Austrian pine takes its place. The Japanese black pine is grown in both areas.

Holly. Yaupon holly stands extreme alkaline soil better than any other holly but finds the winters of central New Mexico too much. However, the Wilson holly (*Ilex altaclarensis* 'Wilsonii') does well here. The Chinese holly (*Ilex cornuta*) should have east exposure here.

Oleander. Grown in El Paso area; treated as an indoor-outdoor plant in Albuquerque.

Privets. Texas privet (*Ligustrum japonicum* 'Texanum') is not reliable. The deciduous California privet and the common privet (*Ligustrum vulgare*) are favorites for hedges here.

THEY GROW WHAT THEY CAN'T GROW

Some of the El Paso nurseries make a liar out of the conventional climate ratings by bringing in and growing a number of plants that supposedly should not be grown in the El Paso climate. Some of them are:

Lemon bottlebrush (*Callistemon citrinus*). Generally damaged at 20°.

Podocarpus macrophylla. Needs protection.

Cape plumbago. Loses leaves and freezes to the ground, but generally comes back quickly from the roots.

Japanese aralia (*Fatsia japonica*). Does fine in a protected patio.

THEY JOIN ALL THE DESERTS IN THE BASICS

Some of the most useful evergreen landscape plants that are successful in both areas are: many kinds of junipers, euonymus, arborvitae (*Thuja orientalis*) and cotoneaster; pyracantha (orange-berried kinds are hardiest); *Photinia fraseri* and *P. serrulata*; gold dust plant (in shade); Oregon grape (*Mahonia aquifolium*); and santolina (both gray and green-leafed kinds).

When it comes to growing deciduous flowering shrubs and trees, the cold-winter areas within this desert win in many ways. The hawthorns do well, and even the goldenchain tree is grown. The flowering crabapples put on a spectacular spring color show. The selection of perennials is almost without limit.

ZONE 11   California's Medium to High Desert

In this climate zone, covering the middle to high elevations in California and Nevada, it is difficult to select any one garden as typical. There is no abrupt line between the low, intermediate, and high deserts of California. The Twentynine Palms area borrows from the low desert, while to the north, Lone Pine and Bishop borrow from the climates of the mountains.

Some of the cities and towns included in this zone, with their elevations, are:

Twentynine Palms	1980'
Las Vegas, Nevada	2006'
Boulder City, Nevada	2525'
Victorville	2858'
Barstow	2105'
Palmdale	2549'
Lancaster	2355'
Ridgecrest	2300'
China Lake	2300'
Edwards AFB	2300'
California City	2400' - 2900'
Boron	2410'
Mojave	2787'

If we take as typical the climates of Palmdale, Lancaster, Mojave, California City, and China Lake, the climate can be measured in the following way.

There is a definite winter season. From December through March, 80 to 85 nights will have temperatures of 32° and below. Low temperatures of 6° to 0° have been recorded, but the mean minimums range from 32° to 28°, with daytime temperatures of 60° and higher.

The advantage of this spell of winter cold is in the successful growing of many deciduous fruits and flowering shrubs that are ruled out in the mild-winter areas of Southern California. Lilacs are popular and do well in this climate. Forsythia doesn't just straggle into bloom; it bursts into a real show of yellow and gold.

LANDSCAPE ARCHITECT: HOWARD FRANKS

Airy blue palo verde trees, desert natives, cast light shade on this livable garden patio.

Actually much planting is done on the basis of the many mild winters rather than the occasional severe ones.

Apples and pears are successfully grown. Peaches and plums are commonly grown, although late frosts may drop the crop of young fruits in some years.

The winter cold is not severe enough to rule out the planting of many plants of marginal hardiness. The oleander may freeze to the ground in the coldest winter, but it goes through most winters with just the outer leaves damaged. The kinds of eucalyptus planted in the past are borderline in hardiness, but a few cold-resistant varieties look promising. Bottlebrush and California pepper are planted, but suffer damage in many winters. Star jasmine and xylosma need a protected place in the garden to survive. The olive finds its outer limits here and is often damaged severely, but recovery is generally rapid.

The summer heat is real, but not to be compared to that of the lower deserts. More than 100 days of temperatures above 90° are expected. Temperatures above 95° average as follows:

April—none in most years
May—from 2 to 7 days
June—from 10 to 22 days
July—from 24 to 30 days
August—from 20 to 30 days
September—from 6 to 20 days
October—less than 7 days

Extremes of 114° have been recorded, and days of 106° to 108° must be planned for in July and August.

RAIN?

Rainfall can't be counted in averages. Annual rainfall of 2 inches or less may occur for years in a row. However, 2 inches of October rain, falling slowly, another 2 inches in November through January, and 2 inches in March—totaling altogether 6 inches—and this desert blooms with a greater variety of wild flowers than any other desert in the world.

The many years of practically no rainfall limit native tree growth to the Joshua tree; the dominant native shrub is the creosote bush.

"OUR WINDS"

In March, April, and May, winds with gusts exceeding 40 miles per hour are a part of gardening. In a windy year there will be 12 to 14 days in those three months with such winds. August, September, and October are the quiet months. Through the summer, winds of lesser velocity come up in the afternoon to blow some of the heat away.

Wind and cold winter considered, the most reliable and useful evergreen shrubs are: euonymus, privet, elaeagnus, photinia, and pyracantha.

ZONE 12   Arizona's Intermediate Desert

This is the garden climate of Tucson, Wickenburg, Florence, Safford.

Here, the high temperatures of the summer months are a few degrees lower than in the low desert gardens. The number of days above 90° is about the same—ranging from 142 to 159.

The number of nights of frost—32° or below—jumps from 10 and 11 in a year to from 22 to 60. Most of these frosts are in the 28° to 32° range. The mean minimum temperature in December, January, and February ranges from 30° to 33°. Infrequent low temperatures, once in 10 years, of 7° to 15° have been recorded.

Here, as in the low desert, spring planting begins in October.

Although the winter temperatures are lower than in the low desert, the total hours of cold are not enough to provide the necessary winter chilling for some of the deciduous fruits and deciduous flowering trees and shrubs.

The winter frosts exclude many of the tender plants of the low desert. But a number of mild winters in a row encourage experimentation, and you see many subtropicals doing very well. Some examples are: the yesterday-today-and-tomorrow shrub (*Brunfelsia calycina floribunda*), Natal plum (*Carissa grandiflora*), the canary bush (*Crotalaria agatiflora*), and calliandra.

Mexican jar, star jasmine, burnt adobe brick wall— *Southwest tradition in Tucson entry court.*

Some of the more or less reliable tender evergreens that reach their limit in cold resistance in this desert are: yellow oleander (*Thevetia peruviana*), *Cassia artemisioides, C. excelsa, C. splendida, Chorisia*, bottlebrush, evergreen pear, bougainvillea, and camphor tree.

The number of natives used in the gardens seems much greater here and in the surrounding high desert than in all other desert areas. Perhaps it is due to the wider availability of natives in the nurseries. Perhaps it is because of the difference in native growth in the surrounding desert.

The rainfall in this area is not much measured in inches—the average is about 10 inches, and half of that comes in the summer months. But those few extra inches make a world of difference in desert growth.

The desert has a different look here. The washes are greenbelts. Elderberry (*Sambucus mexicana*), desert ironwood (*Olynea tesota*), native cottonwood, native hackberry (*Celtis douglasii*), and desert willow (*Chilopsis linearis*) are some of the trees; and in favorable situations they are impressive in stature and structure.

The notorious soil problem in this desert is caused by caliche. (See section on soil management in the following pages.)

Palm Desert garden features plants of zone 13: Washingtonia palm, Aleppo pine, Natal plum.

ZONE 13 Low Deserts of California and Arizona

This is the subtropical desert garden. There are rarely more than 6 to 10 nights with temperatures below 32°. Lows of 19° to 13° have been recorded, but they are infrequent and of short duration. Shrubs and trees that are damaged at those temperatures continue to be planted. More kinds of subtropicals are finding a place in this garden every year.

Where will you find this garden? According to the *Sunset Western Garden Book*, you'll find it in California in such cities as Palm Springs, Borrego, Indio, Brawley, El Centro, Blythe; in Arizona in Phoenix, Casa Grande, Yuma.

From mid-May through September, daytime temperatures may be 100° or higher every day for 6 to 10 weeks or longer. In July, the hottest month, mean maximum temperatures range from 106° to 108°. From October to December, daytime temperatures gradually drop to a mean of 70°, then in February, start their climb to reach 100° in May.

Most planting is planned to take full advantage of the mild winter and very early spring. September and October mark the beginning of the planting season for an unbelievably wide selection of cool weather flowers and vegetables. Growth of the fall-planted plants is slow through the short winter, picks up speed in February, and races through the increasing temperatures of March and April.

The lack of winter cold excludes many of the flowering deciduous shrubs. It's no climate for the hawthorns, and flowering cherries, and deciduous fruit trees such as apples and cherries.

If you would make up a list of trees based upon what you see most frequently as you drive through these gardens, it would go something like this: bottle tree, carob, citrus, fig tree, bottlebrush, jacaranda, olive, and crape myrtle.

And if you were impressed with the unusual, you would add: purple orchid tree, weeping acacia, Joshua tree, Mexican palo verde, and smoke tree.

There are differences in soil and water in this area. All localities using Colorado River water—Indio, Brawley, El Centro, Blythe, and Yuma—have the problem of a fast build-up of salts in the soil unless they do something about it. In these areas periodic leaching of the soil is necessary to prevent accumulation of salts in the root zone. To do the right kind of job of leaching you multiply by three or four the amount of water you would use for a normal irrigation. In many residential sections gardens are laid out so that the entire garden can be flooded to a depth of 4 inches or more. Water comes principally from irrigation district canals, but occasionally from private wells. The water is supplied about every 10 days during the summer, and every 4 to 6 weeks in winter. Local water supplies in Palm Springs and Borrego areas provide a better quality of water, and the problem of salinity build-up is not as critical.

Desert winds

There are several kinds of desert winds.

First, are the spring and early summer wind-and-sand *storms*. You call it a storm when the wind velocity is more than 45 miles per hour, and the sand is mixed with small rocks, and the tumble weeds sail straight through the air.

Then, there are the prevailing winds of varying velocity and duration. In some cases they are mostly afternoon breezes, subsiding shortly after the sun goes down.

And finally, there are the cold high-velocity winter winds.

The extreme sand-laden winds go beyond the ordinary drying, burning, dessicating effect of winds and physically damage trees and shrubs by breakage and by shredding and riddling the leaves.

There is no complete protection from the storms and not much to do about them other than repairing tree stakes, sweeping up the sand, and hosing off the plants.

Windbreaks. The isolated home in the desert, the rancher and the farmer, know the value of windbreaks. In the early planting of desert windbreaks, in California and Arizona especially, the Arizona cypress and the athel tree or tamarisk were and still are the evergreen standbys. The cottonwood, Lombardy poplar, Siberian elm, and black locust are still the reliables of the deciduous trees in every desert climate.

The most effective windbreaks are those planned to lift and divert the wind. They should be wide— 4 to 5 rows of shrubs and trees with about 16 feet between rows. Start with a shrub or small tree on the windward side and build up with medium and taller trees. The first row might be pampas grass, giant reed, or Russian olive; the second row—tamarisk; the third row—Arizona cypress; the fourth row—Lombardy poplar; and fifth row—Aleppo pine.

Where space is limited, a double row of tamarisk and Arizona cypress is most effective.

Winter winds and winter water. Don't minimize the dessicating effect of the winter winds. More evergreens are lost from dessication than from freezing. Remember that in the desert, irrigation is a year-around proposition. The interval between waterings can be stretched, but deep soaking every three to four weeks should continue through the winter.

Wind protection. Wind protection is one thing when your house is exposed to the full sweep of the desert winds and another when surrounding houses and trees give you a wide shelter belt. But even around the house in a tree-covered neighborhood, you can improve your climate by wind-screen plantings, walls, fences, baffles, and overheads. Where prevailing winds are westerly, the northeast corner of the

Like sentinels, Italian cypresses line a boundary and serve as a windbreak in this desert garden.

house gets the most wind protection and the best sun exposure. Plants of borderline hardiness should be located here.

Until you have gardened in a climate where prevailing winds are strong and very prevailing, it is difficult to appreciate the difference in growth between a wind-protected plant and one exposed to the wind.

The hot suns of the desert — how to prevent their damage

Where the sun is really hot, gardeners learn to make changes from the general planting and how-to-grow directions for many plants. Here are some examples:

Hot sun and roses. Roses in desert areas are short-lived when heavily pruned to 3 or 4 canes, 6 to 8 inches high. Here you must prune moderately. With the regular hybrid tea roses, leave 5 to 12 canes, 18 to 24 inches high. This gives you a larger bush that shades the ground.

Floribundas need very little pruning other than to control the height. In beds or hedges where only one variety is planted, prune the plants to keep them uniform in size and height. Thin out the tops and cut them back just enough to encourage new wood to grow in the bush.

Tree roses are generally unsatisfactory in the hottest areas. Even a slight sunburn damage will check growth of stem tissues on the southwest side. Severe burning may crack the bark. Protect with paper or lath.

Climbing roses grow best on east and north sides of the house. If used on the west side, reduce the danger of reflected heat from the wall by growing them on a wooden trellis 6 to 12 inches from the wall.

Effective windbreak-screen is tall, bushy desert gum and low-growing, compact Japanese privet.

Mulching to prevent extreme soil temperatures is a must. (See the section on mulches in this introduction.)

Sun-plus-wind. Every year a good number of deciduous shade trees and fruit trees that are planted bare root are lost due to drying out before and after transplanting. Both the fruitless mulberry and the hackberry need to be handled with special care. If you get your trees early and the trunks are plump and full of moisture, plant and protect them from sun and drying wind by wrapping the trunk with heavy paper, burlap, or at least painting it with a whitewash material such as "tree trunk white". If the trees appear dry, lay them flat in a trench and cover them completely with moist soil or peat moss. In a week or 10 days, they will be ready to plant—with the usual protection.

Citrus trees and sunburn. Citrus trees have bark that is easily damaged by the sun. Injury is most likely to occur on the south and west sides of the tree. Bark becomes hard and brittle and may peel off in large patches.

Not only do young citrus trees need protection, but if the lower skirts of old trees are removed, all exposed areas—trunk and large limbs—should be protected with a whitewash preparation.

How to manage desert soils

In all arid climates, soils have a higher percentage of soluble salts than in those where heavy rainfall leaches the soil (carries the soluble salts downward through the soils and by streams out to the ocean). The hot sun and low humidity through evaporation concentrate salts in the upper layers of the soil. Water used for irrigation may add to the salt content. The manures and fertilizers used in gardening bring in additional amounts.

Excess of salts limits the kind of plants that can be grown, stunts growth, inhibits seed germination, and causes "salt burn"—leaf edges turn brown and wither. The retarding effect on plant growth occurs without any visible damage to the leaves. Plant growth is not as lush; annual shoot growth of affected shrubs and trees is less than normal.

To reduce the salt content in desert soil, you do what nature does in the rainy climates—you pour on great quantities of water periodically to leach the soil. This sounds easy. You have an excess; you get rid of the excess. And it is easy, if the water you use does not contain too much or the wrong composition of the total salts, and if the drainage is adequate.

Every desert gardener should accept the idea that all water contains salts. Furthermore, that unless water moves through the soil, salts will build up in the soil.

The word salts is used to take care of many elements, good and bad. The fertilizers you buy are combinations of salts. And as you well know, an overdose of those beneficial mixtures of salts can kill a plant.

Reading about soils of the desert you meet with the words "saline", "alkali", and "alkaline" in reference to salt content. Confusion arises because technical men in agriculture and horticulture use these terms to describe different kinds of soil problems, while gardeners (and garden books) use them interchangeably. Without trying to straighten out the vocabulary, let's look at the way desert gardeners work with two different soil-water problems.

The gardener in the low desert area of Southern California who uses Colorado River water starts with a soil high in total salts and adds a water that furnishes a ton of salts per acre foot of water a year. This is plainly a saline affair of both soil and water, and the only way to garden is to leach at the start and leach again and again as water is used.

At Palm Springs or any other location in this desert were irrigation water is lower in total salts, the initial leaching might bring the soil into the safety range; and it would remain that way with repeated waterings—if the drainage is adequate.

So, for soils with an excess of salts and water that is high in salts, *leaching* is all the answer you need.

Now look at the problem where neither the soil nor the water contains an excessive amount of salts. Here the trouble comes from water in which the salts are in the wrong proportion. Where the water is high in sodium as compared to calcium, leaching alone does not solve the problem.

Water high in sodium will gradually change the structure of the soil unless a substantial concentration of soluble calcium is maintained. The gardener recognizes the change by a slow-up in soil drainage.

Soils become tight and lose their open structure. Plants that do well the first year are not as successful the second year.

The management of such soils is one of maintaining a balance between soluble calcium and sodium. Fortunately most desert soils are high in insoluble calcium-lime (caliche). So the use of soil amendments such as iron sulfate and sulfur, will acidify the soil and change lime to soluble calcium—the form in which it can prevent sodium accumulation.

This addition of iron and sulfur works wonders in California's high desert areas where well waters are likely to be high in sodium.

And it works again in the correction of caliche soils. (See paragraphs on the special soil problems of caliche and Texas root rot in this section.)

With soils that are low in lime, where sodium is being applied through the irrigation water, gypsum becomes the best soil amendment.

ADD QUANTITIES OF ORGANIC MATTER

There is little organic matter—less than ½ of 1 per cent—in most desert soils. Adding some form of organic matter every time you plant should be automatic in desert gardening.

The purpose of the addition is to improve physically the structure of the soil. That means that you must add enough to break up heavy soils, or to increase the water-holding capacity of light or gravelly soils.

Such materials as peat moss, ground bark, and redwood sawdust should be added in amounts of 30 per cent or more of the soil volume.

For example, in preparing a planting bed, spread a 2 to 3-inch layer of the material over the soil and work it in to a depth of at least 6 inches. The mixing should be done with a rototiller, as thorough mixing with spade or shovel is next to impossible.

Both ground bark and sawdust are now available with nitrogen added. If you use untreated woody material, add extra nitrogen (3 pounds of 20 per cent nitrogen fertilizer, such as ammonium sulfate, per 100 square feet) to compensate for the loss of nitrogen used initially in breaking down the bark or sawdust.

Composted manure is also used as a soil conditioner, but it cannot be added at such high rates without making the soil too hot. Manure breaks down rapidly as compared to other materials and supports increasing populations of beneficial bacteria. When added to other organic material to be worked into the soil, use it at the rate of about 1 to 5 of the bark or sawdust.

There are other advantages in adding organic matter. The soil becomes less alkaline; root rots are less likely to occur; and you have an all-around better environment for root growth.

MULCHES SERVE MANY PURPOSES

In the gardener's language everywhere, a mulch is a loose material—peat moss, ground bark, sawdust, or composted manure—placed over the soil. A mulch can serve any of several purposes: reduce evapora-

Flood irrigation is the most effective way of watering in many desert areas.

Shade is a first consideration in the desert garden—bamboo is an excellent provider.

Crushed gravel is attractive mulch in streetside planting of Aleppo pine and Asparagus sprengeri.

Magnificent mesquite, a native covered with English ivy, gives cool shade to Palm Springs garden.

tion of moisture from the soil, reduce or prevent weed growth, make a garden bed look better, insulate soil from extremes or rapid changes of temperatures.

In the desert garden some of the functions of the mulch are doubly important.

Root-killing heat. When the July sun beats down on the open ground, it can build up soil temperatures to extremes of 108° at a depth of 2 inches; 100° at 4 inches; 97° at 8 inches deep. These are killing temperatures to the roots in the first 4 inches of the soil. A 2 to 3-inch mulch will reduce temperatures by 8° to 10°.

The lowering of temperatures in the top inches of soil is extremely beneficial to plants whose roots—at least a large portion of them—work near the surface of the soil. Plants that should not be cultivated deeply respond remarkably to mulching. Many rose growers add a 3-inch mulch over the entire rose garden. Not only does the mulch allow root growth to continue in the top layers of the soil, but as it breaks down it adds to the humus content.

By maintaining a mulch at the original thickness, adding material as the mulch decomposes or is washed into the soil, the structure of the soil is improved.

More life in the soil. A mulch increases the population of beneficial bacteria. In a soil that is mulched, bacteria find a more uniform moisture content, a more even temperature range, and a constant supply of organic matter—an environment in which they can multiply. This function of the mulch is especially significant where Texas root rot must be dealt with.

Where soil crusts. In many soils, the fine clay particles often create an almost airtight crust over the soil as it dries out after watering. Watering through the mulch, and the insulation of the mulch, prevents crusting and allows free entry of air into the soil.

Where winds blow. Where high winds are a part of desert gardening, the fine-textured mulches such as peat moss, ground bark, sawdust, and manure may be blown around the garden or into another county. Covering them with a layer of coarser material, or pea gravel, or finely crushed rock will keep them in place.

Many desert gardeners are using the decorative bark chunks, either in the large or "acorn" size, as dress-up mulches. Some use them as a layer over a finer mulch; some use them straight.

Mulch in winter? With most plants the mulch is maintained the year around. However, winter damage to plants of borderline hardiness may be increased if the mulch is maintained in the winter months. The winter sun must be allowed to warm the soil during the day so that the reradiation of heat from the soil can lessen the drop of night temperatures.

Some mulches steal nitrogen. Sawdust and ground bark, unless they have been fortified with nitrogen at the mill, will rob the soil of nitrogen in the first stages of decomposition. To make up for this loss, fertilize once for the mulch and once for the plant when you spread the mulch. Follow up with your regular feeding program in slightly heavier amounts the first season.

Garden and desert separated only by low adobe brick wall. Century plant overshadows small lily pool.

CHLOROSIS

Chlorosis—the lack of normal green color in the leaves—is widespread throughout all desert areas. This physiological disorder is commonly attributed to the lime in the soil fixing the trace of iron necessary for green color in plants and making it unavailable to the plants. In caliche soils the "lime-induced" chlorosis is common. But chlorosis is frequently seen in valley soil very low in lime. Just plain unfavorable growing conditions such as waterlogged soil, low soil temperatures, poor drainage, and lack of organic matter, can cause this disorder.

Chlorosis is most pronounced in the youngest leaves of the growing tips. In a mild case, the leaves show normal green veins with paler green areas between. In a moderate case, both the leaf blade and the veins are a pale green or yellow and the growth is stunted. In a severe case, the entire leaf becomes yellow or white and the leaf margins turn brown. Chlorosis is treated in many ways. No matter what the cause, the first step is to prevent excess water, either by regulating the watering or by providing drainage.

All treatments include the application of iron in some form. Iron chelates give the quickest results as

the iron is in a form that cannot be fixed in the soil. Spraying the leaves with a liquid iron solution is also effective since the leaves take up the iron regardless of the soil conditions.

One of the treatments recommended by the University of Arizona for roses goes like this:

"Supply soluble iron to the plant roots by making holes in moist soil in the root area from 3 to 6 inches deep. Put in each hole a heaping tablespoon (about 1 ounce)of ferrous (iron) sulfate and cover with soil. Apply ½ to 1 pound per bush (about ¼ to ½ cupful) depending upon size of bush. Each irrigation will diffuse enough soluble iron to the adjacent portions of the root system to supply the plant. One treatment is usually effective for 2 to 4 years. Marked recovery usually occurs within a month after treatment."

Another treatment that gives quick response but requires care and skill is to insert the iron directly into the rose canes. In canes ½ inch or larger, bore a hole not over ¼ the diameter of the cane, to the center of the cane. Fill with iron citrate and close the hole with tree paint.

Large shrubs and trees are often treated in the same manner. The larger the tree, the more holes can be bored. Don't let the size or the number of holes weaken the tree.

The best cure is prevention. In preparing new planting beds, remove the existing soil to a depth of 24 to 30 inches and make up your own planting mix. Add about 30 per cent organic matter. Work in a complete fertilizer according to label directions. To each cubic yard of soil, also add 1 to 2 pounds of iron sulfate. Mix thoroughly.

CALICHE

Caliche (pronounced cal-*lee*-chee) is a good technical word. It is derived from the Latin *calx*, meaning lime. The Spanish in the southwestern United States used the word to designate the calcerous hardpan formations in the desert soils, and soil scientists still apply this term to such deposits.

Deposits of caliche may be at the soil surface, or from a few inches to several feet below ground level. The thickness also ranges from several inches to many feet. The accumulation can be granular, or cemented into compact, impermeable layers.

Caliche is not a problem in deep soils of the valleys. But in locations outside the valleys where the caliche is covered by little or no soils, it is a real problem.

The best solution where the deposits are thick and tight is to bring in heavy equipment—a trencher or a backhoe—and remove the stuff to make way for a soil mix in which plants can be grown. If you can't dig deep enough to get drainage, the only answer is to plant above the caliche in raised beds or large planters.

Some gardeners dig round holes; some dig cross-shaped ones; some dig trenches. Whatever the shape, make them large enough to take all the soil the plant will need from youth to maturity. Without drainage out of the hole, no hole is large enough.

Soil mixes to replace the caliche should have an extra supply of iron. The same mix as developed in the sections, "Add quantities of organic matter" and "Chlorosis", is satisfactory for refilling planting holes. However, in the case of caliche, you start with an imported soil and then add the organic matter and iron.

TEXAS ROOT ROT—SOIL TREATMENT

There is a great similarity between the soil treatments to correct chlorosis, to plant in caliche, to check development of Texas root rot, and just to make sick plants well again. The treatment of the soil for Texas root rot would be beneficial to the growth of plants in any condition.

This root rot is caused by a fungus that destroys the outer portions of the roots, thus cutting off the water supply to the plant. The first sign of the disease is a sudden wilting. When this happens at least 50 per cent of the root system has been damaged.

This fungus is favored by a highly alkaline soil that contains very little organic matter. Fortunately, the fungus does not compete well with other soil-inhabiting organisms. Therefore, control measures are aimed at reducing alkalinity by adding sulfur and increasing the populations of organisms that are antagonistic to the fungus by adding organic matter that decomposes rapidly.

You can attempt to save a damaged tree this way: Drill holes 2 to 3 feet deep and spaced 3 feet apart in a wide band around the drip line of the tree. Fill the holes with a mix of manure, sawdust, and soil. If using manure only, don't go higher than 10 per cent of the mix. If using sawdust make a mix of 1 to 5. To a yard of mix add 5 pounds of sulfur and 1 pound of ammonium sulfate. Or, you'll get quicker action by using iron sulfate instead of sulfur, or by combining 4 pounds of sulfur and 2 pounds of iron sulfate. Blend the mix well and fill the holes. Water deeply.

Since the root system is damaged, prune back and thin to remove half the foliage.

When planting in soils suspected of being infected, dig extra wide and deep planting holes and use the same soil mix as outlined above for backfill around the root ball.

Living in close contact with natural surroundings is especially possible in the Southwestern deserts. This Arizona home overlooks the expanse of Paradise Valley, echoes the desert in its plantings of saguaro and prickly pear cactus among rocks.

LANDSCAPING PLANS AND IDEAS

Landscape architecture, the arrangement of space for use and beauty, implies that the planner must first have a good acquaintance of his surroundings and know how he wants to live in them.

The first impression one has of most desert gardens is that they are simple and direct in comparison with the typical home garden in other regions. An expanse and boldness seems to echo their surroundings—the great Western deserts.

To you as the garden architect, the desert area offers many possibilities. You may choose to have an informal garden with an authentic desert flavor and take advantage of low-maintenance desert native plants. For the many Southwest home owners who have moved into a suburban area on the edge of the desert, there are especially strong arguments for using native plants: They belong there, they need little care, and most are hardy.

On the other hand, you may prefer to transform the desert into an oasis of your own liking, creating your own surroundings. If you live in a town house and desire the lushness that few desert plants can give you, a few kinds of imported non-native plants —used with restraint, and carefully maintained and controlled—may be the answer. The important thing in landscaping is not which approach you take, but that you have imposed some order on nature, that the garden is the result of a predetermined plan with a purpose. This chapter is intended to help you establish that basic plan.

Landscape architecture is a marriage of art and nature. The relationship is a distinctive and complex one, as you know if you are familiar with the peculiarities of the desert. Hopefully, the ideas pictured here will give you the start, the final touch, or guide you completely through the creation of your garden in the desert.

Demonstration home garden

Those who live or visit in the Tucson area have an added opportunity to receive information and inspiration in planning their desert gardens. The Desert Museum—*Sunset Magazine* Demonstration Desert Garden in Tucson Mountain Park was established to demonstrate ways in which home owners can achieve more livable and easily maintained gardens in the desert climate.

Native plants only. Plantings here are limited to trees, shrubs, vines, perennials, and annuals found in the states of Arizona and Sonora, Mexico.

In the demonstration garden, you can see how desert plants adapt to garden situations—some of these wildlings outshine commonly planted non-native ornamentals. Most important in an arid climate, native plants get along with less water—and rarely need feeding and spraying.

Native desert plants are becoming more available in nurseries. Growers around Phoenix and Tucson, and also Palm Springs, California, are beginning to build up a supply. About half the plants are in containers, and half are sold directly from private desert grounds.

The best time to plant desert natives is in the fall or early spring. Get them well started before the heat arrives.

Structural materials. Another purpose of the garden is to demonstrate a variety of structural materials in different uses. Paved surfaces now include exposed aggregate, etched concrete, and brick. There are walls of burnt adobe brick, exposed aggregate, concrete block covered with stucco, and native rock.

LANDSCAPE ARCHITECT: GUY S. GREENE

Wing-like ramada provides shelter in Demonstration Desert Garden in Tucson.

In dramatic silhouette from foot of steps leading from carport to patio in Scottsdale garden is Camelback Mountain. All plants are natives.

Sheltered by huge boulders, pool in Carefree, Arizona *seems to have occurred naturally in its setting. Beige paving, flagstone coping enhance illusion.*

Exposed aggregate of concrete steps approximates weathered desert rock. Rosemary spills over rocks.

Natural sites

All landscape composition must be attached to some particular piece of ground; therefore, the design should be influenced by and grow out of the peculiar characteristics of the site itself. The Southwest desert, more than any other environment we know, seems to call for gardens that are natural and straightforward in planning, as those pictured here.

Pool at the desert's edge among boulders

Like a pocket of aquamarine locked in stone, the pool on a rocky bluff in Carefree, Arizona pictured here is striking enough to draw you down from the garden above for a look, even if you're not going for a swim.

What compels attention is how it seems so much at one with its site. The designers, Toyo Nursery for Thomas D. Darlington, took great pains to fit the pool into a natural location among the boulders, and to use a paving with color and texture as close as possible to that of the native rock. Set on a ledge a level below the main grade, the pool area also forms a visual transition from the bright greens of the main garden to the more subdued hues of the

"Desert wash" is framed by ocotillo, red gum, and different kinds of cactus.

Living room window looks out on garden in harmony with the open desert beyond it.

desert. The planting, in a mixture of humus and the on-site decomposed rock, cascades down a wall, or fills in a pocket here and there, to relieve the starkness of the natural rock.

A desert wash in a Phoenix garden

In the Phoenix garden pictured above, a transition is achieved between two levels by simulating a desert wash. The bold forms of the plants growing at the edge of the wash contrast effectively with the other plants in the garden. The landscape designer used river-washed pebbles along the edge of the wash, and coarse gravel in the center. Large native rocks give an additional natural effect to the wash and its plantings.

They pushed back the desert

Anxious to retain the Southwestern flavor of their home and property in Tucson, the owners of the swimming pool on this page in a sense pushed back the desert to make room for the pool, and at the same time, encouraged the desert to grow up close around it—actually replacing with natives wherever the desert growth was a little too sparse.

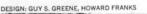

From pool you look across desert toward Tucson. Lights dramatize desert plants at night.

Dramatic forms of ocotillo and cactus contrast with Natal plum, roses (right), and serve as transition between desert and garden.

DESIGN: ANDRE CUENOUD, E. F. FRAZIER

Growing by wall: fan palm, bottlebrush, Carolina cherry laurel, yellow oleander, roses, bauhinia.

Natives and exotics

The Phoenix garden pictured on this page is a successful compromise joining native plants with lush, green imports.

You'll find azaleas (both shrubs and standards), junipers, a fan palm, bird of paradise (*Strelitzia reginae*), and *Ficus benjamina* (above roof line) growing near the main entrance. Off to the right, *Podocarpus macrophylla*, wisteria, and roses grow in the planting bed beside the second entry. Tifgreen Bermuda grass lawns, used extensively throughout the garden, are overseeded in the fall with a fine-leafed fescue for a green turf in winter. Round concrete stepping stones serve as paths, and crushed gravel makes a neat mulch in many planting areas.

Non-natives

Unlike most of the desert gardens in this chapter which use native plants in abundance, there is little in the garden on this page to suggest that it is only minutes away from the arid, open desert.

The reason is simply that the owners who moved to Tucson a few years earlier from the San Francisco Bay area, wanted a green, lush garden reminiscent of their former home.

The strongest single influence in this garden is Japanese. You find it in the lantern, the Ming urn (planted with a Japanese black pine), the stone figure, the reed insets in the fence in the sideyard, the roofed gate, and the use of rock. Mondo grass (*Ophiopogon*), bamboo, camellias, hibiscus, and papyrus (not shown in the photographs) are all plants commonly associated with Japanese gardens and adapted to the desert climate.

River rock seeded in concrete gives bold texture to entry path. Loquat on left, camellias in pots.

LANDSCAPE ARCHITECT: JOSEPH S. FOLKNER

Patio is patterned with dichondra, paths. Photinia, Aleppo pine, weeping mulberry, bamboo against fence, pine in urn. Patio is left of entry shown above.

Sunny open spots are for cool winter days; others with filtered shade are welcome in summer.

Beauty and utility

Landscaping is the development of property for use as well as beauty. Thus it has both utilitarian and aesthetic aspects. In the West especially, the gardener is concerned with being able to *use* his garden, to "live in" the out-of-doors. This new kind of landscaping has not evolved as a style. Call it site planning, or land use, or landscaping; it is planning the garden for use by people. Therefore, in planning the landscape, the desert gardener should strive to create schemes that are original and pleasing to the eye and which fit into our present-day way of life.

A refreshing recessed garden

Lowering this small garden in Scottsdale, Arizona, brought about these results: greater privacy, some protection from the wind, and a feeling of being set apart from the surrounding desert area.

A small tractor equipped with blade and scoop was used to cut an irregularly shaped area about 18 inches deep, with gently sloping sides. At the center a deeper cut created the basin for an informal, refreshing pool.

The garden's African daisies, poppies, sand ver-

Feeling of space comes with grade change and open area covered by pea gravel. Bank outlines garden.

LANDSCAPE ARCHITECT: LOIS BENEDICT

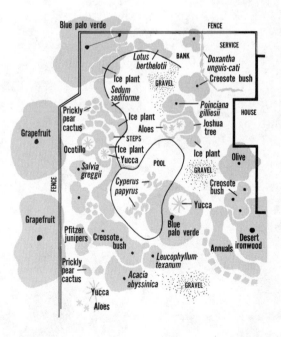

The plan of the garden indicates the types of plants that are used.

bena, and sweet alyssum are annuals that reseed regularly. Desert mallow and penstemon, which are both perennials, and creosote bush (*Larrea*), a native evergreen shrub, give seasonal color and permanent green background. Sharp forms of aloes, cactus, and ocotillo remind you that you are still in the desert.

The desert sweeps right up to the garden wall

This hillside garden a few miles north of Tucson is obviously a garden to enjoy, not one to labor in. Several low-maintenance areas provide for the activities of this family: There is generous paved space around the pool for sitting or sunbathing, a shady ramada nearby for outdoor dining, a round paved terrace in the back with a fire pit for cool winter days or chilly evenings. From this back terrace, the family can enjoy the sunsets and desert twilight and, after dark, watch the lights of Tucson in the distance.

This garden blends impressively with its surroundings; the desert sweeps up to the house in a natural way. There has been no attempt to move in large quantities of cactus and rock; neither has the character of the desert been denied. The cultivated garden plants in beds adjacent to the house add a certain refinement and cool greenery, but do not act as a barrier to blot out the surrounding landscape.

Fire pit attracts family for coffee break and marshmallow roast on cool winter day.

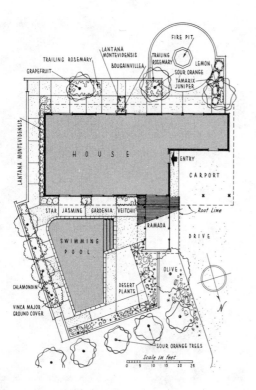

Cultivated plants here number about a dozen, and these are close to the house for easy watering.

DESIGN: GUY S. GREENE & ASSOCIATES

Circular terrace juts out into the desert from house like a great bay window.

Low maintenance

A popular characteristic of the desert garden is that it can be very easy to take care of.

The architect of the inviting garden on this page limited the maintenance requirements in several ways. The developed garden occupies only a small portion of the area available; the rest was left in its native state, studded with existing desert growth that requires no maintenance at all. Within the garden, lawn area was kept small, generous use was made of

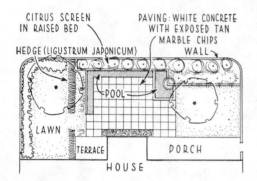

Water spilling from pool to pool and lush green plantings create oasis effect in desert garden.

Plan shows only portion of maintained garden directly behind house; rest is left to desert growth.

From living room you look at raised beds, pools and water plants. Olive provides filtered shade.

Garden framework and plants carefully planned by the architect for low maintenance.

patio paving, and plantings were carefully chosen.

The rear garden of the Arizona home in the two pictures on the right was redesigned to provide a spacious yet easily maintained planting area that would stay attractive through all seasons.

The owners decided to install waterproofed redwood screens to hide the parking strip and children's play area, to add a small patio and garden outside the master bedroom, and to raise the level of that portion of the lawn that is adjacent to the main patio for an effect of greater space.

A wide concrete curb separates the garden levels so the family can use the patio and raised lawn terrace even when the lower lawn is being flood-irrigated. The extended curb footing serves as a step, and also makes lawn mowing and edging easier. The garden beds and lawn on the upper level are watered by a system of bubblers and sprinklers.

Dark gray, almost black Mexican beach pebbles were chosen as the ground covering in the bedroom patio area. With their uniform large size, they add bold texture to the transition area between the planting bed and the concrete patio.

To keep garden chores to a minimum, only a few annuals and perennials are grown in flower beds. Seasonal color is provided by pyracanthas, oleanders, yuccas, and showy crape myrtle.

LANDSCAPE ARCHITECT: JOHN C. AVERILL

Neat planting around bedroom patio includes crape myrtle, shiny xylosma, trailing rosemary, yuccas.

Desert plants mean low maintenance. This entry planting is in Arizona.

View from patio. Palo verde grows behind screen that hides parking and storage area.

Filling in the details

Pictures on these two pages will give you a closer look at the basic elements comprised in good desert landscapes. The plant groupings here, mostly entry and streetside plantings, were obviously selected with careful consideration for pleasing relationships of form, foliage texture, and color. In desert landscapes especially, the grouping of plants is important in determining how much maintenance your garden will require and whether or not you can cultivate that tender plant successfully.

Companion plants are night-flowering cactus, Mexican fan palms, yucca, low-growing lavender lantana.

DESIGN: ROY MORIUCHI

Oriental effect is achieved with fence and narrow planting bed in Glendale, Arizona garden.

DESIGN: CONTEMPORARY LANDSCAPE COMPANY

Desert plants in containers like Yucca aloifolia, loquat are popular, hardy in cold weather.

Rocks are nucleus for dwarf Natal plum, creeping rosemary, Yucca aloifolia. *Dodonaea against wall.*

Selection of accessories is important too. Notice how much at home rocks are in desert gardens.

Gravel mulches prove extremely useful to streetside plantings. They add a well groomed touch and serve effectively to conserve moisture and prevent growth of weeds.

Most important, note that the plants pictured are adapted to existing climate and soil conditions. If they couldn't take heat, drying winds, and alkaline soil and water, their beauty would count for little. The use of some particular types of plants are discussed further in the following chapters of this book.

ARCHITECT: ARTHUR T. BROWN

Cow tongue cactus looks sculptured against burnt adobe wall topped with concrete blocks.

Illumined at night, desert plants take on a new and fantastic kind of beauty, look softer, more gentle.

Feathery wormwood senna, creeping rosemary thrive next to house in sunny Phoenix garden.

DESIGN: HOWARD FRANKS, GUY S. GREENE

Multiple trunks of olive tree are handsomely silhouetted against wall of Tucson home.

TREES FOR SHADE AND WIND CONTROL

You can hardly overstate the importance of trees and their beneficent influence on a desert environment. Obviously, many pioneer settlers were aware of this when they planted trees for shade and as windbreaks around their homes and ranches.

The choice of trees by the early settlers was based on two requirements: Will it grow? Will it give shade or wind protection next year or the year after?

Throughout all desert climates the deciduous trees that met these requirements of survival and fast growth were the cottonwoods, poplars, Siberian elms, black locusts, and China-berry trees; the evergreens were the athel tamarisk, Arizona cypress, and Aleppo pine. In the low deserts the list widened to include more evergreens such as beefwood, black acacia, and eucalyptus.

Today's desert gardeners can choose from a much longer list of trees. And the list will continue to grow as new trees are tested and proved desert-worthy. But when choosing trees, don't sneer at these old-timers. If your home happens to be one alone against the desert, they may be your best bets—at least in your first plantings.

Choice of trees is greatly influenced by where they will be used. If the tree is to be added to a garden that is now reasonably well protected by neighboring house and trees, you have a wider choice than if it is used in an unprotected situation to tame the wind and sun.

A look at the best sellers

Deciduous trees most frequently planted for shade and wind control in all desert areas

The mulberries

Fruitless mulberry (*Morus alba*—fruitless varieties 'Cutleaf', 'Mapleleaf', and 'Stribling' are identical. 'Kingan' is reportedly hardier). The fruitless mulberries are the most frequently planted trees in the desert by a wide margin. Fast grower (to 20 feet high and as wide in 3 to 4 years). Gives dense shade. Roots are not invasive if watered deeply. Prune by thinning out and shortening branches to a well

placed, upward-growing bud. Do not prune heavy branches to stubs.

The ashes

The Modesto ash is by far the most widely planted of the ashes. It is a selected form of the native Arizona ash (*Fraxinus velutina*) with light green, shinier leaves.

Another form of the Arizona ash called fantex ash (*F. v.* 'Rio Grande') is a new addition to the list of ashes. It has larger leaves.

Other ashes that are now available and being tried out are: Marshall seedless green ash, and the blue ash.

The thornless honey locusts

The development of selected forms of the thornless honey locust (*Gleditsia triacanthos inermis*) has added several excellent shade trees to the desert's list.

Moraine locust. Fast-growing, deep-rooting, wide-spreading.

White mulberry is deciduous to 60 feet. The fruitless forms are most desirable.

Spacious and shady Tucson garden features Aleppo pine, yucca, young oleander hedge. Bermuda lawn overseeded with annual rye for green turf in winter.

DESIGN: NICK PONOMAREFF

29

Sunburst honey locust in Sedona has fernlike foliage with bright yellow tips resembling flowers.

Texas umbrella tree, a variety of China-berry, is a favorite shade-giver in desert areas.

Shademaster locust. More upright than the moraine and even faster growing.

Sunburst locust. New foliage is golden yellow. Open and irregular growth.

The flowering locusts

Black locust (*Robinia pseudoacacia*). Rough, thorny, and rather sparsely branched; but if shaped and pruned, it is a handsome tree with its white flowers in hanging clusters.

Idaho locust. Large, deep rose flowers in clusters.

Pink flowering locust. Fragrant, pale pink flowers.

The cottonwoods and poplars

It is surprising how many different poplars are now being grown in the deserts. The early plantings were mostly the native cottonwood (*Populus fremontii*) for shade, and the tall-growing Lombardy poplar for windbreaks. Now one wholesale tree grower distributes 4 different cottonwoods and 6 poplars.

The extremely fast growth and ease of propagation have made these trees deservedly popular. You can plant a windbreak or a grove of shade trees by cutting branches in late winter, sticking them in the ground where they are to grow, and you have a new tree come summer.

The invasive root system of the poplar makes it a difficult tree to live with in a small garden or where there are sewer lines. But for windbreaks in a hurry and shade trees in basins in dry-ground gardens, the poplars are hard to beat. Some kinds available are:

Cottonless cottonwood. Propagated by cuttings from a male tree. The female cottonwood bears masses of cottony seeds.

White cottonless cottonwood. Very white bark. Called a hybrid in Mojave desert.

White poplar (*P. alba*). Wide-spreading. Leaves are white-woolly underneath.

Bolleana poplar (*P. a.* 'Pyramidalis'). Narrow columnar form.

Carolina poplar (*P. canadensis*). Narrow spread.

Balm-of-Gilead (*P. candicans*). Wide-spreading.

Lombardy poplar (*P. nigra* 'Italica'). Tall, columnar, with upward-reaching branches.

The elms

The name Chinese elm has been attached to two different elms. The elm that you see most frequently in desert areas is the Siberian elm (*Ulmus pumila*), one of the hardiest, toughest trees known to man. To be that, it is both deep-rooted and shallow-rooted. Its seeds sprout like weeds throughout a moist garden. As a windbreak tree it grows fast where other trees fail; and if planted in an area where only trees are grown (and watered in basins), it's a good tree.

The true Chinese elm (*U. parvifolia*) is not as extremely hardy as Siberian elm, but is well adapted to all desert zones. However, it remains evergreen in the warmest winters only. As a garden tree it is much easier to live with than the Siberian elm.

The sycamores

California sycamore (*Platanus racemosa*). Large, picturesque tree. Smooth branches often gracefully twisted and contorted. Attractive when trained into multitrunked clump. Nurseries offer singles, doubles, and clumps.

Arizona sycamore (*P. wrightii*). Similar to California sycamore. Scaling bark. Trunk often white. Leaves more deeply lobed.

American sycamore, or **buttonwood** (*P. occidentalis*). Strong-growing and wind resistant. Maplelike leaves.

Sawleaf zelkova is nearly 60 feet tall with equal spread. Thick turf grows right up to base.

Young silk trees shade driveway, screen home from street, will later form broad canopy.

European sycamore (*P. acerfolia*, often sold· as *P. orientalis*). Both the American and the European sycamore have the same habit of growth and the same maplelike leaves. The new bark of the American is whiter, and the tree is out of leaf longer. These sycamores are excellent in formal plantings. When planted 15 to 20 feet apart and top-pruned to spread wide, they will quickly create an overhead canopy.

The willows

Where there is plenty of water, the weeping willow makes a big statement in the desert. Desert pioneers appreciated the willow's fast growth and ease of growing from cuttings. Many kinds are available:

Weeping willow (*Salix babylonica*). Most commonly planted.

Wisconsin weeping willow (*S. blanda*). Not as weeping as above.

Globe Navajo willow. A large, very tough and hardy, round-topped tree.

Three kinds of pussy willows are offered: the small gray, the fluffy gold, and the gold red.

The China-berry

The variety Texas umbrella tree (*Melia azedarach* 'Umbraculifera') is an old favorite in desert areas. Its dense, spreading, dome-shaped crown gives deep shade. Lilac flowers in May are followed by ½-inch, yellow, hard, berrylike fruits. Should be pruned regularly to maintain umbrella shape.

Deciduous shade trees, less frequently planted but well adapted

Many nurseries hesitate to bring in trees that are new to their surrounding areas. It is natural that most home owners choose from trees they have seen and admired in the area around them. So, generally, the list of available trees tends to perpetuate itself.

The following deciduous trees vary in popularity by locality depending upon how well they have been demonstrated locally.

Silk tree, mimosa (*Albizia julibrissin*). Hardy all zones. Fast growing, it luxuriates in the desert heat. Grows as a multitrunked tree with low, wide-spreading, arching branches, unless trained early as single stem and staked. Powder puff pink flowers in July and August.

Chinese pistache (*Pistacia chinensis*). Hardy zones 10, 11, 12, 13. Slow and awkward growing in the first years, then moderate to fast growth to make a handsome, durable, wide-spreading tree. An excellent lawn tree is headed high. The only tree in the desert to color scarlet in the fall.

Japanese pagoda tree (*Sophora japonica*). Hardy all zones. Fairly fast growth to 25 feet, then slow. Deep-rooted and giving light-filtered shade, it's a good tree to garden under. Yellowish-white flowers look like sweet peas.

Sawleaf zelkova (*Zelkova serrata*). Hardy all zones. Fast growing to 40 feet or more. Leaves similar to those of the elm. Recommended as a substitute for the Siberian elm. Seedling trees vary in growth habit and need to be pruned carefully when young to create a strong framework. Selected forms, propagated from unusually well formed individual trees, are becoming available.

Chinese jujube (*Zizyphus jujuba*). Well adapted in zones 10, 11, 12, 13, especially 10 and 11. Deep-rooted and salt-tolerant, it takes everything the desert has to offer. Small yellowish flowers in clusters in May and June are followed by shiny, reddish-brown, datelike fruits that have a sweet applelike

Aleppo pine, resistant to drought, wind, grows quite fast; these in Tucson are five years old.

flavor. Dried and candied, they resemble dates. From every viewpoint it's a good desert tree.

The evergreen trees of wide adaptation

Pines for the desert

Interest in pines took a big upswing a few years ago when landscaping in the Japanese manner became popular. Pine trees were looked at, not just as trees that grow fast or slow, but as plants with form and structure. As a result, more pines and more kinds of pines were made available.

Gardeners in the Southwest deserts have been more cautious in trying out new pines than gardeners in the natural pine country, but several pines new to the desert have been admitted.

For years the most satisfactory, and most frequently planted pine in both the high and low deserts has been the Aleppo pine (*Pinus halepensis*). And it still holds that honor. The Aleppo may not be the most beautiful pine in the world, but so far no other pine equals it in reliability and speed of growth under desert conditions. When established with a trunk 3 inches or more in diameter, it stands straight against the prevailing wind without too noticeable distortion of foliage. The Aleppo pines are quite individualistic in growth habit. Usually the tree is an informal or narrow pyramid with branches to the ground in its first years, becoming more rugged as it ages.

A new variety is now available—in small sizes only. It is labeled *P. halepensis* 'Brutia'. Reportedly it has the same growth habit as the species, but the needles are twice as long, more rigid, and darker green.

The Japanese black pine (*P. thunbergiana*) is proving well adapted in every desert climate, and now

is generally available. It's a good pine with rocks, or in gardens with large areas of gravel or pebbles. Easy to train, it's the favorite of the pruning-shears sculptors.

Another pine that does well in both the low and high deserts is the Digger pine (*P. sabiniana*). This pine that looks so sparse and straggly in the dry foothills, is a beautiful pine when grown under garden conditions. It's fast growing when consistently watered.

The slow-growing pinon pines are finding their way into more high desert gardens. Some nurseries offer aged, collected nut pines (*P. edulis*). Cones contain edible seeds (pine nuts). Unfortunately the tree doesn't bear cones until about 20 years old. The Mexican pinon pine (*P. cembroides*) is the most treelike of the pinons. The singleleaf pine (*P. monophylla*), a shrub-tree of great character, is seldom available in nurseries, although it is the most common native pinon in Southern California.

The Italian stone pine (*P. pinea*) is slower growing in the high desert than the Aleppo, but it is equally well adapted to desert conditions. It becomes a stout-trunked tree before it is 6 feet high. You'll get greater height quicker if you do not prune to the umbrella-branched shape too early. Cut back the lower branches, but do not remove until the tree grows to the height you want.

Coulter pine (*P. coulteri*) is one of the utility pines of the Mojave Desert. It's much slower growing than the Aleppo pine but equally well adjusted to desert conditions. Wide-spreading branches to the ground may make it too wide for the small garden. It is particularly good-looking alongside an irrigation ditch.

Trial plantings of cluster pine (*P. pinaster*) in the high desert are doing very well in their fourth year from 5-gallon cans.

There's a strange pattern in the adaptability of pines to the deserts. Pines that are native in coastal areas, such as cluster pine and Torrey pine (*P. torreyana*) are better adjusted than pines that grow a few miles away at slightly higher elevations, such as ponderosa pine (*P. ponderosa*). The pines that thrive best are the pines native to the Mediterranean region or southern Europe—the Aleppo and the stone pines.

In growing pines in the desert, remember that, like all evergreens, they can be damaged severely by dessication when in the path of cold winter winds. Watering through the winter months is essential.

To many pines, however, water is an essential hazard. The Monterey pine (*P. radiata*) for example, is not recommended for the desert because of losses through root rot. The water mold fungi that cause root rot thrive and multiply in overly wet soil. Normally you can live with the water molds by watering

Red gum (Eucalyptus camaldulensis) *serves as wind-break, screen in Scottsdale garden.*

DESIGN: DAVID J. WOOD

Arizona cypress screen on side of house. Selected forms are uniform in size, shape.

infrequently but deeply. But infrequent water is hard to manage when summer heat puts the tree under stress.

A better solution, and recommended for all pines in trouble from root rot or chlorosis, is to improve drainage by boring deep holes with a post hole digger around the tree and filling them with a mix of half peat moss or ground bark and half soil. Add a high nitrogen fertilizer if the tree has not been fertilized lately. If the tree is chlorotic, add iron sulfate or iron chelate.

All pines can be shaped, and usually improved by pruning. If you wish to slow down the growth or to make a rangy pine more compact, cut back the candles of new growth when new needles begin to emerge. Cut them back halfway or even more. If you want growth to continue along the branch, leave a few clusters of needles.

The cypresses

Arizona cypress (*Cupressus glabra*). All zones. Valuable and much used as a tall screen or windbreak. Fast-growing, deep taproot. Seedlings vary in form and color. If planting a hedge or tall screen where you want uniformity, look for one of the several selected forms. 'Gareei' has silvery, blue-green foliage; 'Pyramidalis' is compact and symmetrical; 'Compacta', more globe-shaped.

The tamarisks

Athel tree (*Tamarix aphylla*). All zones except cold areas of 10X. They look sad when temperatures drop near 0°. Recovery from trunks or roots is rapid. Commonly used for windbreaks and planted by the mile. Easy to grow from 1 to 2-inch-thick cuttings, set in place and kept watered. Dramatically fast growth. Has both deep and shallow-spreading roots. When used near other trees or garden plant-

ings, lateral roots should be pruned occasionally to within 4 feet of the trunk.

Salt cedar (*T. pentandra*). This deciduous tamarisk substitutes for the athel tree in the cold area of 10X. It bears tiny pink flowers in dense clusters in summer. Can be maintained as a flowering shrub if cut back to the ground in early spring.

The eucalypts

The low and intermediate deserts (zones 12, 13) have a good assortment of the reliable eucalyptus trees. A number are grown in zones 10 and 11, but with some winter damage and the threat of severe winter damage in the occasional deep freeze. The high deserts could use more tall-growing, fast-growing evergreens; trial plantings of hardy varieties continue.

Some of the eucalypts that have given good performance in the mild-winter areas and fair performance in the high deserts are:

E. camaldulensis. Tall and mighty. Hardy 12° to 15°.

E. microtheca. Bushy, round-headed tree to 35 to 40 feet. Hardy 5° to 10°. Strong-looking, strong-growing. Doing very well in zones 12, 13. Worth trying all zones.

E. polyanthemos. Slender; erect to 30 to 60 feet. Hardy to 14° to 18°.

E. rudis. Large shade tree to 30 to 60 feet. Hardy 12° to 18°.

E. viminalis. Tall-spreading, patriarch tree if soil is deep. Hardy to 12° to 15°.

Other relatively hardy eucalypts worth trying: *E. nicholii*, 12° to 15°; *E. pauciflora*, 10° to 15°; *E. macrandra*, 8° to 12°.

Magnolia

Southern magnolia (*M. grandiflora*). All zones except cold areas of 10X. Evergreen. Don't plant it where it must take the full brunt of the wind. Needs to be consistently watered and fertilized. Used as a lawn tree.

The hardy pepper

Peruvian pepper (*Schinus polygamus*, formerly *S. dependens*). All zones except the cold-winter areas of 10X. It lacks the green, lacy gracefulness of the California pepper, but is a cleaner tree as far as litter is concerned. It is more upright in growth and hardier than the California pepper. When planted 4 feet apart it will quickly make an almost impenetrable hedge or screen.

Olive

An historic landmark of the Spanish southwest, *Olea europaea* is found in zones 12 and 13. It is not reliably hardy in zones 10 and 11, but continues to be planted there. It suffers light winter damage at 12°, and is killed to the ground at 6°. Most trees will sprout from the base after a killing freeze and make sizeable multitrunked trees in a few years.

Trees for the warm-winter deserts only

Purple orchid tree (*Bauhinia variegata*). Zone 13. Wonderful show of light pink to orchid-purple flowers, usually from February to April. There is a white form.

Lemon bottlebrush (*Callistemon citrinus*). Safe in zones 12, 13; often suffers winter damage in 10 and 11. Noted for bright-red, 6-inch-long brushes. Nurseries offer it as a shrub, an espalier, or a tree.

Citrus. Many kinds. Oranges, grapefruit, limes, mandarins, tangerines, tangelos. Standard varieties of oranges are grown in the low California desert. Best home garden oranges in Arizona are Dillar and Hamlin. (See the special chapter on citrus.)

Purple hop bush (*Dodonaea viscosa* 'Purpurea'). Zones 12, 13. Large evergreen shrub or trained as a small tree. Can be pruned as hedge or espalier, or planted 6 to 8 feet apart and left unpruned to become a big, 12 to 15 foot high, informal screen.

Coral tree (*Erythrina*). Large deciduous shrubs or trees noted for their spectacular show of brilliant flowers from greenish-white through yellow and orange to red. There are at least a half dozen kinds adapted to zones 12 and 13.

Jacaranda. Deciduous or semi-evergreen tree limited to zone 13. Fairly hardy when mature. Young plants may be killed back at 25°, but often come back to make multistemmed shrubby plants. Tree grows to

European olive is decorative in Tucson lawn. Algerian ivy spreads over planter beneath tree.

25 to 40 feet. Bears clusters of lavender-blue flowers, usually in June.

African sumac (*Rhus lancea*). Zones 12, 13. Slow-growing evergreen to about 25 feet with an open-spreading habit. Attractive dark green foliage. You can train it to a single trunk or let it grow as a multi-trunked tree. Or train it as a tall screen or clipped hedge. In areas where many other trees become chlorotic, it remains green.

California pepper tree (*Schinus molle*). Hardy in zones 12, 13. Fast-growing to 25 feet or more and as wide as it is high. This beautiful lacy evergreen is not for a small, tidy garden that must be kept neat and clean. Plant it where its falling leaves and berries can decorate the ground and its roots won't crack pavements or invade sewers, and it's a great tree. Makes an attractive hedge if planted 2 to 4 feet apart and trimmed to any height between 4 and 8 feet.

Carob, St. John's bread (*Ceratonia siliqua*). Zone 13. Large evergreen shrub or tree. Can be used as a multistemmed large hedge. Normally it maintains a bush form with branches to the ground. Trained as a tree with lower branches removed, it grows at a moderate rate to become a round-headed 20 to 40-foot tree.

Spring flowering trees

Gardeners in the high deserts have a much wider choice of spring-flowering deciduous trees than their

California pepper tree casts filtered shade all year in Phoenix garden. Prickly pear in foreground.

Purple orchid tree (Bauhinia variegata) *displays peak spring bloom shading patio in Phoenix.*

neighbors in the low deserts. Flowering fruit trees, for example, give a very sad performance after a warm winter. They stagger into a light show of flowers and leaf out very late.

Each spring-flowering tree has its own requirement for winter chilling. The flowering cherries have the highest requirement. The purple-leaf plums have the least. The flowering peach and crabapple are in between.

The purple-leaf plum (*Prunus cerasifera*) and its varieties—'Krauter Vesuvius', 'Thundercloud', and 'Hollywood'—are well adapted to both the low and high deserts. 'Hollywood' is a hybrid with a fruiting plum and in addition to a good show of flowers produces good quality plums, 2 to 2½ inches in diameter.

The dwarf red-leaf plum (*P. cistena*) grows as a dainty, many-branched shrub; or it can be trained as a single-stemmed tree. At its best in zones 10X, 10, 11.

The flowering crabapples are surprisingly tolerant of desert conditions. Although they are at their best in cold-winter areas, flowering crabapples are grown with fair success in all deserts.

The exuberant display of the flowering peach makes it the favorite in the high deserts. It needs to be severely cut back after flowering to maintain it as a giant bouquet.

Trees for shade and fruit

The high deserts provide enough hours of winter chilling to allow the standard varieties of apples, pears, peaches, plums to lead a normal life. In the low and intermediate deserts (zones 12, 13) many varieties fail to leaf out in a normal fashion, and to produce a normal crop. Gardeners in these deserts should skip apples, pears, and cherries.

Peaches are grown successfully *if* varieties with a low chilling requirement are planted. Choose early-ripening varieties such as 'Blazing Gold' and 'Gold Dust'. Such familiar standard varieties as the 'Elberta', 'J. H. Hale', and 'Hale Haven' are generally unsatisfactory.

Nectarines grow vigorously and blossom beautifully, but few trees produce satisfactory crops of edible fruits.

Several varieties of plums produce good quality fruit. 'Santa Rosa' is the best choice if you are planting but one tree. 'Santa Rosa' is a good pollenizer for the early-ripening 'Beauty', the flowering-fruiting 'Hollywood', and the 'Mariposa'.

The oriental persimmon grows well but fruit production is uncertain. The only variety recommended is 'Hachiya'.

Figs find the low desert to their liking as evidenced by the huge old trees growing along irrigation ditches. The 'Mission' variety will produce 2 or 3 crops a year.

Almond trees grow to make picturesque shade trees, but they are not consistent in nut production. Two varieties must be planted if you want to try for a nut crop. 'Ne Plus Ultra' and 'Nonpareil' are recommended as a good team.

SHRUBS THAT TAKE DESERT EXTREMES

Here we take a look at the plants—shrubs, vines used as shrubs, trees used as shrubs—that occupy the garden in the various levels beneath the tree level.

Our main concern here is their use in the garden: as ground covers of varying heights; as hedges and screens for privacy and climate control; as edgings for borders, walks, and driveways; as foundation and wall plantings; as giant bouquets; and as container plants for patios.

Plants of many uses—rated high in home landscaping

If you visited a thousand gardens in the deserts and made a list of the shrubs (and the plants used as shrubs) seen in those gardens, the 14 plants in the chart on the next page would be at the top of the list. A thousand gardeners could do a wonderful job of landscaping with these few plants without any two gardens looking alike.

To earn a place on the most-frequently-used list, a plant must have these qualities:

. . . widely adapted

. . . easy to grow

. . . need no special protection where adapted

. . . easy to maintain at a size that fits its location

. . . good all year performance or attractive over many months

. . . good backgrounds (medium to tall shrubs) for the transient color of bulbs, annuals, perennials, flowering shrubs.

Of course there are many other shrubs with these qualities; but before discussing them, let's take a quick look at the plant favorites listed in the chart.

Silverberry (*Elaeagnus pungens*). One of the toughest, hardiest evergreen shrubs. Can take the reflected heat of a west wall and any amount of wind. Will grow into a 15-foot-high shrub, but can be trained in any fashion to any height and thickness by regular pruning.

Euonymus. These are cast iron evergreens where both cold resistance and heat tolerance are important, and where soil conditions are unfavorable. Mildew is sometimes a problem even in the desert,

so don't plant in corners with poor air circulation.

There's a form for almost every purpose. Box-leaf euonymus (*E. japonica* 'Microphylla') makes a compact, formal, low border or small hedge. *E. japonica* will grow to 8 to 10 feet with a 6-foot spread, but it is generally seen pruned or sheared to 3 to 4 feet. The many variegated varieties—green edged white, or gold, or with yellow centers—do not fade out in the desert sun. Purple-leaf winter creeper (*E. fortunei*) has a sprawling growth habit and is used as a ground cover. There are varieties of euonymus that serve well as espaliers, such as *E. f.* 'Sarcoxie' and *E. kiautschovica* 'Manhattan'.

Junipers. Almost all of the low-growing, ground cover type junipers give a good account of themselves in the desert if consistently watered. The spreading junipers that completely shade the ground do better than the open growers. You have a wide choice of forms in the shrub-type junipers — vase-shaped, arching, dense upright, irregular upright. The dependable, large-growing pfitzer (*Juniperus chinensis* 'Pfitzeriana') is the most frequently used of the large, arching shrub types. Armstrong juniper is more compact and more formal-growing than the pfitzer. The Hollywood juniper (*J. c.* 'Torulosa'), upright-growing with irregular twisted column appearance, is frequently used as a strong accent plant.

Juniper softens the wall; prostrate rosemary grows in front of the rock.

'Victory' pyracantha in full flower, trained as pillar plants in Phoenix garden. They thrive though exposed to hot sun, reflection from concrete blocks.

NAME	CLIMATE ZONES	GROUND COVER	LOW BORDER	HEDGE	SCREEN	FOUNDATION PLANTINGS	ACCENT—GOOD FORM	ATTRACTIVE WHEN MASSED	BACKGROUND PLANTINGS	TRAIN AS SMALL TREE	FRUITS	FLOWERS	HOT SOUTH OR WEST WALL	EAST OR NORTH WALL	TAKES SHADE
Silverberry (*Elaeagnus pungens*)	all			●	●	●			●		●		●		
Euonymus	all	●	●	●	●	●								●	
Juniper— Low growing	all	●				●		●					●	●	
Juniper— Shrub types	all			●	●	●	●	●	●					●	●
Photinia	all			●	●	●	●		●					●	●
Privet (*Ligustrum*)	all			●	●	●			●	●		●	●	●	●
Pyracantha	all	●		●	●	●		●	●		●	●	●		
Roses	all	●	●	●		●	●	●				●		●	
Rosemary	all but coldest 10X	●	●			●		●				●	●		
Santolina	all		●			●		●				●	●		
Star jasmine	best in 10, 12	●				●		●				●		●	●
Arborvitae (*Thuja*)	all			●	●	●	●						●	●	●
Wisteria	all								●	●		●	●	●	
Xylosma	best in 10, 12, 13			●	●	●			●	●			●	●	

Photinia. The Chinese photinia (*P. serrulata*) will grow to 35 feet but is easily held to 8 feet by pruning. *Photinia fraseri* is not as vigorous in the desert climates; but its showy, bright, bronzy-red new growth makes it the popular choice. For evergreens both have unusual cold tolerances. Both take the heat and wind, but they look better and grow faster when planted on the east side of the house.

The privets. Four kinds are used throughout the deserts. The Japanese privet, or waxleaf privet (*Ligustrum japonicum*) is dense-growing to a height of 10 to 12 feet if not pruned. Excellent evergreen for hedges, screens, or shaping into formal shapes. Texas privet (*L. j.* 'Texanum') is lower-growing and has somewhat denser foliage. The glossy privet (*L. lucidum*) is the one seen as a round-headed tree. It can be grown as a large shrub, or multitrunked tree, or planted 10 feet apart as a tall screen. California privet (*L. ovalifolium*) is the hardiest privet and evergreen only in the mildest winters. Fast growth to 15 feet but can be held to any height by frequent pruning.

Pyracantha. Wide choice of forms and berry color. The hardiest are the varieties of *P. coccinea*, especially the orange-berried 'Lalandei'. Two are low-growing and wide-spreading, suitable for ground covers: *P.* 'Walderi' and *P.* 'Santa Cruz'. Use the tall-growing as espaliers on fence or wall, as barrier plantings, screens, rough hedgerows or barriers along rows. Can be trained as standards or clipped into a formal hedge.

Roses. As providers of masses of color over the long summer—from May through summer and fall—it's hard to beat the floribunda roses. Some of the most satisfactory varieties are: 'Heat Wave', 'Ivory Fa-shion', 'Summer Snow', 'Circus Parade'. Use them in masses of one variety in beds and borders.

Rosemary (*Rosmarinus officinalis*). The most frequently used rosemary is the semi-dwarf variety 'Lockwood de Forest', or sometimes labeled 'Santa Barbara'. Growing to about 2 feet high and spreading to 4 to 5 feet, it serves many purposes—a ground cover, a spiller to drape over a low wall, an attractive companion to rocks, or a wide border. Attractive all year with bright-green narrow leaves and clusters of lavender-blue flowers in winter and spring. Can be clipped to create a flat surface. Should be thinned out and pruned now and then to prevent woodiness. Takes hot sun plus reflected heat.

Lavender cotton (*Santolina chamaecyparissus*). Reliable, amenable to shearing, this 2-foot-high, wide-spreading, gray shrub can play many roles. Plant it 3 feet apart as a bank or ground cover; plant it 1½ to 2 feet apart as edger for walks, borders, or foreground plantings.

The green santolina (*S. virens*) is similar in growth habit, but leaves are narrower and deep green. Both santolinas remain attractive longer if held to 1 foot or less by regular clipping. Plants open up and expose dry stems if allowed to grow normally.

Star jasmine (*Trachelospermum jasminoides*). This star performer as a vine or sprawling shrub should be given a choice location in entry garden or patio where it will get relief from the hottest sun and where its fragrance may be enjoyed. Excellent ground cover under trees that need summer water.

Arborvitae (*Thuja*). The arborvitaes that take desert conditions without a whimper are varieties of the Oriental arborvitae (*Thuja orientalis*). You see them

Versatile pyracantha as hedge on south side of house, kept at 3 feet by pruning only twice a year.

Draping santolina's gray foliage contrasts with green and reddish leaves of Nandina domestica.

Espaliered xylosma is trimmed monthly in this Tucson garden to keep it flat.

widely used around foundations; as pairs or groups by doorways or gates; in formal rows. There are many forms from dwarf golden globes, to golden and green columns, to tall-growing pyramids. Juvenile foliage is needlelike; mature leaves are scalelike in flattened sprays carried vertically. Some varieties carry the juvenile foliage throughout their life. 'Rosedalis', growing to a 4-foot globe, has green, needlelike foliage.

Probably the most popular is the dwarf golden arborvitae, labeled 'Aurea' or 'Berckmanii' or 'Aurea Nana'. It grows as a compact, golden globe to about 3 feet.

'Raffles' is more compact, more golden, and smaller than 'Aurea'.

'Fruitlandii' is a compact, upright grower with deep green foliage.

Wisteria. A most adaptable woody vine that can be trained as a big shrub, a single-trunked tree, or a multistemmed, semi-weeping tree.

Ready-trained tree wisterias are now available bare root as well as in containers. The Japanese wisteria (*W. floribunda*) produces the longest flower clusters, which open gradually from the top. The Chinese wisteria (*W. sinensis*) opens nearly to the full length of its 12-inch flower clusters.

Xylosma. Best in zones 10, 12, 13. This doesn't look like much as a young plant in the nursery. And it is frustratingly slow to take hold and grow after planting. In spite of these drawbacks it has grown in the affection of gardeners and landscape architects to become one of the top favorites among the landscape structure plants. You know why when you see its clean, yellowish-green foliage shining in the hottest sun. It really thrives in the heat. If left alone the plants develop an angular main stem that takes its time zigzagging upward. Meanwhile, side branches grow long and graceful, arching or drooping. Easy to train as an espalier or as a small tree.

Contenders for top honors among the basic landscape plants

If you were surprised by the omissions in the charted basic list on page 38, consider the basis for inclusion in the list. These are not necessarily the *best* landscape shrubs. They are, at the present time, the 14 *most frequently used* throughout the desert areas. There are many plants of equal merit that are not quite as easy to grow or not as versatile, or more specialized in climate adaptation, or perhaps just not as well known. We talk about such choice landscape plants in the lists that follow.

(Remember that these are the plants used in landscaping in the conventional manner—arranging an oasis in the desert. If your interests are in the desert-type, low-maintenance garden, the chapters on landscaping and natives will interest you.)

Glossy abelia (*Abelia grandiflora*). All zones. A tall-growing evergreen or partially deciduous shrub with graceful arching branches—if not sheared to a hedge form. In warm-winter areas it makes an attractive screen. A dainty-looking plant with a rugged constitution.

Dwarf coyote brush (*Baccharis pilularis*). Adaptation to all desert climates is not known. Has lived through a 0° winter in zone 11 without losing its shiny cheerful look. A native to the California coastal areas that has surprised desert gardeners with its excellent performance in extreme heat and cold.

One plant will spread to 6 feet or more, or drape that distance down a wall or bank. Planted 3 feet apart it will make a dense, rather billowy mat of bright green made up of small, ½-inch leaves closely set on many branches. Must be pruned every spring to keep growth low and even. Cut out old arching branches and thin to encourage new growth.

Luxurious growth of Bougainvillea 'Barbara Karst' *increases feeling of verdancy in this courtyard.*

Barberry (*Berberis*). All zones. There are numerous kinds—evergreen, deciduous, low growers, tall growers. Enthusiasm for them varies by the climate. Where winter temperatures may drop to 10°, the evergreen Darwin barberry adds a valuable 3 to 6-foot shrub to a short list of hardy evergreens.

The Japanese barberry (*B. thunbergii* 'Atropurpurea') is useful as a hedge or barrier planting. It's deciduous, but its attractive bronze-red, then purplish-red foliage all summer long earns its keep in the eyes of many gardeners. The dwarf form, 'Crimson Pygmy', growing to 1½ feet in ten years, makes the brightest low edging you have ever seen. Bright-red new leaves change to a bronzy blood red.

Bougainvillea. Zones 12, 13. These spectacular, shrubby vines can't be rated as reliably hardy but that doesn't bother gardeners in low and intermediate deserts. Some of the hardiest varieties that have been successful in the desert are:

'Barbara Karst'. A vigorous tall grower, bright red in the sun, bluish-crimson in shade. It blooms young and gives color over a long season.

'San Diego Red', 'Scarlet O'Hara', 'American Red'. Hardiness is equal to the old fashioned purple kind. Deep red color over a long season. Vigorous and tall-growing, it can be trained as a small tree by staking and pruning.

There are a number of varieties of shrublike growth that are effective in containers, in the shrub border, or wherever you want a blaze of color. Some of the shrubby ones are:

'Temple Fire'. It's a partially deciduous shrub to about 4 feet high with a 6-foot spread. Color is called bronzy-red.

'Crimson Jewel'. Shrubby and sprawling and of lower growth than 'Temple Fire', and some say that it has a "better" color.

'La Jolla'. Shrubby and compact. Bright red. It's a natural for container growing.

Natal plum (*Carissa grandiflora*). Zone 13. Although leaves are damaged when temperatures drop below 20° and the plant must be considered borderline in this area, it is seen in many sizes and forms. There are a number of low-growing varieties that serve beautifully as ground covers. 'Green Carpet' grows to 1 to 1½ feet and spreads to 4 feet or more. 'Prostrata' stays under 2 feet and is vigorous and wide-spreading. 'Tuttle' is somewhat taller growing and spreads to 5 feet.

Cocculus laurifolius. This evergreen shrub or small tree thrives in zones 12 and 13, either in full sun or deep shade. Usually grown as a large multistemmed shrub but can be espaliered.

Cotoneaster. All zones. How many of the many cotoneasters will grow well in each of the deserts may never be known. There are too many kinds of cotoneasters. The two that have proved desert worthy in all of the deserts are:

Silverleaf cotoneaster (*C. pannosa*). Evergreen or half evergreen in coldest winters. Erect-growing with small gray leaves on arching brances to 8 to 10 feet. Clusters of bright-red berries in winter. Silverleaf is attractive only when it has room to develop its natural fountainlike growth. Makes a rugged informal screen.

Red clusterberry (*C. lactea* or *C. parneyi*). A very handsome evergreen shrub with graceful arching habit. Grows to 6 feet with a spread of 8 feet. Dark green, rather leathery leaves and brilliant red fruits, October to December. Foliaged to the base, it is useful as informal screen or pruned into formal hedge.

In the high deserts (zones 10X, 10, 11), the low-growing, ground-hugging kinds come into their own.

Attractive entry walk in Palm Desert garden is lined with dwarf Natal plum.

Cotoneaster as a ground cover—peg down or cut off upright-growing branches.

Purple hop bush is grown as a hedge in this garden at Palm Springs.

Good companions are tamarix juniper, nandina. Bamboo stake fence, rocks give Oriental effect.

Hop bush *(Dodonaea viscosa).* The native Arizona hop bush is fairly common in southern Arizona at elevations from 2,000 to 5,000 feet. It is probably hardier than the plants available at nurseries which are introductions from Australia. The purple hop bush is most frequently used. It is fast growing to 12 to 15 feet and almost as wide, with many upright stems clothed with willowlike bronzy-green leaves. Makes an attractive informal screen.

Pineapple guava *(Feijoa sellowiana).* Best in zones 12, 13; borderline in 10, 11. Hardiest of the so-called subtropical fruits. Grows normally as a large, many-branched, gray-green shrub, but can take any amount of pruning or training to almost any shape: espalier, screen, hedge, or small tree. Performs best when planted in shade or partial shade.

Wilson holly *(Ilex altaclarensis* 'Wilsonii'). All zones. Evergreen. Usually a 6 to 8 foot shrub but can be trained as a small tree. One of the best hollies for the desert areas. Use as a patio tree, shrub, screen, or clipped hedge.

Yaupon *(I. vomitoria).* All zones. Evergreen. Shrub or small tree with small dark green leaves that invite shearing. Stands extreme alkaline soils better than other hollies.

Dwarf yaupon *(I. v.* 'Nana'). A durable and attractive shrub of compact growth to about 18 inches high and twice as wide. A good grower.

Myrtle. All zones except cold areas of 10X. True myrtle *(Myrtus communis)* grows to make a 5 to 6-foot, rounded shrub, or eventually a 15-foot multi-stemmed tree; or it can be held to 3 feet by pruning. It is an attractive individual when allowed to have its own way. You can appreciate its good structural quality by lightly pruning to reveal its main branches.

Dwarf myrtle *(M. c* 'Compacta') is smaller-grow-

ing, more compact with densely set small leaves. It's a favorite for edging, formal hedges, foundation plantings.

Heavenly bamboo *(Nandina domestica).* Looking at this plant you wouldn't expect it to be tolerant of extremes of heat and cold. It does lose some of its leaves at 10° and may be killed to the ground at 0°, but it recovers quickly from the roots. It is not a bamboo, but is reminiscent of bamboo in its lightly branched, canelike stems and delicate, fine-textured foliage. Will grow to 8 feet but can be held to 3 feet by pruning old canes to the ground.

Useful in narrow, restricted areas, or where light, airy effects are called for. Give it a place where it will get enough sun to bring out its reddish fall and winter color, but protect it from the hottest sun.

Periwinkle *(Vinca major).* The large-leafed variety is the one for tough situations in the desert. This trailer, with its dark green leaves and lavender-blue flowers, does a beautiful and practical job as a ground cover in relatively small areas. Looks its best in part shade but holds up in full sun if watered frequently and generously. To keep the ground cover smooth and fresh looking, shear the plants close to the ground occasionally.

Tobira *(Pittosporum tobira).* All zones except cold areas of zone 10X. A broad, dense shrub to 6 to 15 feet unless pruned back. (Should not be sheared; reduce height by selective pruning of branches.) Foliage of leathery, dark green leaves is clean-looking at all times.

The variegated variety with its green leaves outlined in white stands out beautifully from darker greens in a shrub border. It is smaller-growing—to about 5 feet.

Carolina cherry laurel *(Prunus caroliniana).* Zones 10, 11, 12, 13. Makes a densely foliaged upright

Variegated tobira, creamy green, stands out in sun or shade. Grows into informal hedge in full sun.

shrub to 20 feet, or trained as a tree it will reach 30 feet or more. Useful as a tall screen or clipped hedge. The variety 'Bright 'n Tight' is lower-growing, more dense, more luxuriant foliage.

Giant summer bouquets

Newcomers to desert gardening soon learn that there are many wonderful plants that properly should be labeled "heat-loving" rather than the negative-sounding "heat-tolerant".

In truth, the desert gardener has more summer-flowering shrubs to choose from than does the gardener in the mild-summer climates.

Take a look at the shrubs in the following list. All flower with gusto through the summer months; they not only tolerate the heat of July and August, they thrive on it.

Of course these are not the only shrubs or trees that bring color to summer gardens. Check through the list of native trees and shrubs in the Natives chapter, and note the good providers of summer color: desert willow, desert honeysuckle, Texas ranger, and the spectacular yellow trumpet flower.

Butterfly bush or summer lilac (*Buddleia davidii*). This old-timer grows like a weed in the desert. Best when cut back to the ground in winter whether it loses its leaves or remains evergreen. Will grow fast to bloom in summer months. Many color forms: deep pink, reddish purple, blue, red, white.

Pampas grass (*Cortaderia selloana*). All zones. Pampas grass is a plant you like to look at in a neighboring yard or along a roadway or grouped in an acre-sized lawn. Along about September when it carries its 1 to 3-foot-long, white plumes on stalks above a fountain of grassy leaves, it's a great flag-waving plant. But it's not a plant for the small garden. It can

become a monster that is most difficult to cut back to size. Some gardeners control it by burning it to the ground every year or two. However, its indestructableness makes it valuable in windbreaks, large bank plantings, areas difficult to care for.

Crape myrtle (*Lagerstroemia indica*). All zones. Whether you call it a large shrub or a tree depends upon where you live. It is easily grown as a tree in zone 13. More often as a large shrub in zone 12. Suffers occasional winter setback in 10 and 11. Needs protection of warm wall in cold areas of 10X. Crape myrtle is one of the most generous suppliers of color in the summer months. Crinkled flowers in clusters near or at ends of branches, in shades of red, rose, pink, orchid, purple, and white.

Oleander (*Nerium oleander*). All zones. Thriving in the desert heat, it is in full color almost continuously from June to October. In zones 12 and 13, it can be trained as a small, single-stemmed or multitrunked tree. In 10, 11, and the warm-winter areas of 10X, it is grown as a large shrub. Cold winters may damage outer leaves and some branches, but recovery is fast in the heat of early summer. Many color selections.

Bird of paradise bush (*Poinciana gilliesii*). Zones 10, 11, 12, 13. A native of South America that does so well in the desert that it has escaped cultivation and is called a native. It's evergreen or deciduous depending on winter cold. Fast grower to 5 to 12 feet. Very attractive filmy foliage on a rather open, angular branch structure. Clusters of yellow flowers adorned with bright red stamens. Bloom all summer long.

Border of pampas grass has dramatic background of red cliffs in Arizona's rim country.

DESIGN: ANDRE CUENOUD

Yucca and yellow oleander combine well alongside house in Phoenix garden.

Bird of paradise bush is interesting but not dominating garden subject.

Rose of Sharon or shrub **Althaea** (*Hibiscus syriacus*). All zones. This hardy old-timer serves best where winters are cold. In summer it carries single and double flowers to 3 inches across in a wide range of colors—white, pink with red eye, red, purple. To keep plant young and to get larger flowers, cut back (in winter) previous season's growth to 2 buds.

Perennial hibiscus (*H. moscheutos*). All zones. Largest flowers of all hibiscus, and they laugh at desert winds. Each year stems start growing from the ground as late as March and make a 4 to 6-foot shrub (with giant flowers) by July. Bloom continues through the summer. Some varieties are: 'Giant Raspberry Rose', 'New Blood Red', 'Ruffled Cerise', 'Super Clown'.

Pomegranate (*Punica granatum*). Zones 10, 11, 12, 13. The dual purpose pomegranate—red flowers followed by burnished red fruits in the fall—is the fruiting variety 'Wonderful'. Can be grown as a 12-foot fountain-shaped shrub or as a small tree if trained early. In areas so high in sodium that no fruit trees will grow, pomegranate leads a normal fruitful life.

Spanish broom (*Spartium junceum*). Zones 10, 11, 12, 13. Appreciated for its display of fragrant bright yellow flowers from May to August. Out of bloom, it is a compact collection of almost leafless green stems. Grows fast to 6 to 10 feet.

Yellow oleander (*Thevetia peruviana*). Zone 13 and (with protection) 12. An evergreen shrub that thrives in the heat but can't take much frost. Features fragrant, yellow to apricot flowers in clusters through the summer. Must be protected from wind. In warm winter areas can be grown as a 20-foot tree, or pruned to 8-foot hedge or screen.

Chaste tree (*Vitex agnus-castus*). All zones. A large-growing deciduous shrub that enjoys hot summers. Showy, 7-inch spikes of lavender-blue flowers in summer and fall. The chaste tree combines well with other big shrubs—bird of paradise bush and red, pink, or white crape myrtle.

Some good tub shrubs

Growing plants in containers has many advantages and one big disadvantage — the responsibility of keeping the containers watered.

This disadvantage is a minor one when growing annuals through fall, winter, and spring. But when plants are grown on a year-around basis, watering becomes a demanding chore in the summer months. Some enthusiastic container gardeners arrange to include the containers in their automatic irrigation systems.

In some ways, growing plants in large containers is the final denial that you are gardening in the

---

**FORSYTHIA, LILACS, SPIRAEA, MOCK ORANGE...
SPRING COLOR IN HIGH DESERTS ONLY.**

In the high desert there's enough winter chill to trigger the opening of buds of deciduous flowering shrubs and trees that perform miserably in the warm-winter desert climates.

Visit high desert gardens in the spring and you'll enjoy the color of flowering quince, forsythia, mock orange, lilacs, deutzia, many viburnums including the old snowball.

desert. You disregard the native soil and plant in an artificial growing mix that is tailored to fit the plant. And you locate the plant in the spot that modifies the climate to the greatest extent.

Take the case of the camellia for example. The camellia produces larger flowers in areas with high summer temperatures than in cool coastal climates. So you plant it in a "soil" made up of straight peat moss and sand or perlite. Then locate the container where it will get light but not hot sunlight and feed with an acid-reacting fertilizer such as a commercial camellia-azalea food.

Gardenias are grown in containers in the same fashion (in zones 12 and 13) except they require more sunlight—a filtered sun.

Success with plants that require an acid soil is dependent not only on a special soil mix, but on a good quality of irrigation water.

Shrubs with polished, neat foliage that gives that well-groomed, aristocratic look are at their best when well cared for in a container protected from the suns and winds that burn. Some examples:

Burford holly (*Ilex cornuta* 'Burfordii'). All zones. Glossy, leathery leaves; large, bright-red berries. The varieties 'Burfordii Nana' and 'Dazzler', more compact and smaller growing than the species, are excellent in containers. Require protection from hot sun. Plant on east or north side of house if not growing in containers.

Japanese boxwood (*Buxus microphylla japonica*). All zones. This is the boxwood most commonly used for low clipped hedges in shady areas. Often trimmed as a pyramid or globe when grown in containers on shady patio.

Sweet olive (*Osmanthus fragrans*). Zones 12, 13. Will grow to 10 feet or more but can be held to 3 or 4 feet and shaped to suit your fancy. Glossy 4-inch-long leaves hide small flowers of powerful, sweet, fruity fragrance. Protect from hot sun.

Holly-leaf osmanthus (*O. heterophyllus*). Zones 10X, 10, 11. The variegated variety with densely set leaves edged in white is slow growing to about 4 feet.

Aucuba. Hardy all zones. The variegated varieties are usually slower growing. A bulky, buxom shrub, densely clothed with polished leaves. Grows in the deepest shade where other plants fail.

Japanese aralia (*Fatsia japonica*). Grown in tubs in protected patios in zones 10, 12, 13. Tropical appearance with big, glossy, deeply lobed, dark green leaves.

New Zealand flax (*Phormium tenax*). All zones as a perennial. All year performance in zones 12 and 13. Made up of many swordlike, stiffly vertical leaves in a fan pattern. Dwarf forms are available.

Eleven vines for wall covers—patio shade

Coral vine, queen's wreath (*Antigonon leptopus*). Best treated as a perennial in all zones except 13. Fast growing. Revels in high summer heat. Will quickly grow from roots to shade patio. Rose pink flowers in long sprays.

Bougainvillea. See landscape shrubs.

Common trumpet creeper (*Campsis radicans*). All zones. Deciduous. Strong vigorous grower. Good patio vine. Trumpet-shaped, 3-inch long, orange-red flowers in clusters, May through September.

Grape. All zones. 'Thompson Seedless', 'Perlette' and 'Ribier' are easy to train on arbor.

Jasmine. Several evergreen species are used in zones 12, 13.

Honeysuckle (*Lonicera japonica*). Evergreen. All zones. The variety *L. j.* 'Halliana' is most frequently planted. Strong grower.

Virginia creeper and **Boston ivy.** Deciduous. All zones. Virginia creeper (*Parthenocissus quinquefolia*) has looser growth than Boston ivy (*P. tricuspidata*) and can be used to drape over a trellis, as well as clinging to a wall. Both do best on east or north wall.

Flame vine or **golden shower** (*Pyrostegia venusta*). Evergreen. Zone 13. Tubular orange flowers in fall and winter. Thrives in heat. Good for west wall.

Cape honeysuckle *Tecomaria capensis*). Evergreen. Zones 12, 13. Brilliant orange-red tubular flowers in October and through winter. Needs support to make a wall vine.

Wisteria. See list of 14 basic landscape shrubs.

Hall's Japanese honeysuckle covers slope, prevents erosion in this Apple Valley, California garden.

Graceful Jerusalem thorn filters sun over driveway in Phoenix garden. This native requires minimum attention once established, produces bright yellow flowers in May.

NATIVE TREES AND SHRUBS

The shrubs and trees native to the Southwest deserts divide themselves into two groups: Those that have found special ways to survive under extreme drought conditions; and those that grow in the desert but require a normal, or near normal, amount of water to survive.

Some of the desert natives in the need-water class are so widely distributed by nurseries that they have lost the "native" label. Examples are: Arizona ash, Arizona cypress, California sycamore, Fremont cottonwood. In the list of native trees that follows in the next section, those that are in the need-water class are: desert willow, desert elderberry, netleaf hackberry.

The fascinating natives are those that are specially equipped for arid desert survival. To study the many ways these plants have found to fight for survival is an education in gardening.

Many conserve moisture by reduction in leaf size. The palo verde trees are examples of such drastic leaf reduction that the function of photosynthesis must be taken over by the branches.

Coating leaves with varnish-like substances is another method of preventing water loss. Note the creosote bush.

Under extreme drought conditions, many natives simply shed their leaves and go dormant until water is available again. The ocotillo does this dramatically.

The palo verdes, ironwood, creosote bush, and mesquite trees have deep taproots to reach deep water, and lateral surface roots to absorb light rains.

The gray or silver color of many of the drought-resistant shrubs and perennials is due to various kinds of protective devices—a waxy coating on the leaves (as with brittlebush), or fine velvety hairs, or a whitish meal, or scales. Gray is the color of many introduced drought-resistant ornamentals that are well adapted to desert conditions. For example: the indestructible shrub-tree, Russian olive (*Elaeagnus angustifolia*), and santolina, dusty miller, and *Teucrium fruticans*.

Native trees

Elephant tree (*Bursera microphylla*). Zone 13. Deciduous tree to 20 feet. Crooked branches taper rapidly and, to some observers, resemble elephant trunks.

Blue palo verde (*Cercidium floridum*). Zones 10, 11, 12, 13. Deciduous. Fast-growing (in gardens) to 25 feet and as wide. In spring, clusters of bright yellow flowers almost hide the branches. Its tiny leaves are shed early, leaving bluish-green leaf stalks, which with the many branches and branchlets lightly filter the sun. A great tree.

Littleleaf palo verde, or **foothill palo verde** (*C. microphyllum*). Zones 10, 11, 12, 13. Deciduous. Branches and leaves yellow-green. More compact, more spiny than the blue palo verde.

Mexican palo verde, horse bean, Jerusalem thorn (*Parkinsonia aculeata*). Zones 10, 11, 12, 13. Fast-growing at first, then slow to 15 to 30 feet. If you want a high-branching shade tree, young trees must be staked and trained. Foliage is sparse. Branches are slender, spiny, spreading, often pendulous.

Desert willow, willowleaf catalpa (in New Mexico and Texas it's **mimbre** or **flor de mimbre** (*Chilopsis linearis*). All zones. Deciduous. A graceful small or large tree from 8 to 24 feet. Bears small trumpet-shaped, fragrant flowers in white, lavender, pink, or rose from July through August. Commercial tree growers are making selections of colorful individuals and propagating the selected forms.

Smoke tree (*Dalea spinosa*). Zones 12, 13. Deciduous. Usually grows to about 12 feet, but with water in the summer grows in bursts to 30 feet. Good show of fragrant violet-blue flowers in April through June. (The "smoke tree" that's hardy in zones 10X, 10, 11 is *Cotinus coggygria*, a shrub-tree. Its puffs of purple smoke come from large, loose clusters of fading flowers.)

Smoke tree has network of ashy gray branches, with indigo blue flowers April through July.

LANDSCAPE ARCHITECT: LOIS BENEDICT

Western catalpa provides generous shade in areas where summers are hot and dry.

Blue palo verde, native to Arizona, southeastern California, casts filtered shade in Scottsdale.

Grove of wide-spreading native mesquite trees shades patio and choice cactus planting in Phoenix garden.

Common hackberry, deciduous to 80 feet, is ideally suited to desert climate soils.

Netleaf hackberry, palo-blanco (*Celtis laevigata reticulata*). All zones. Large deciduous tree to 30 to 40 feet and spreading wider than it is high. Makes an excellent shade tree if consistently watered.

Huisache, sweet acacia (*Acacia farnesiana*). Zones 12, 13. Large deciduous shrub or tree to 20 feet with equal spread. Gives a good show of deep yellow flowers, January to April.

Native shrubs

Big salt bush, or **quail bush** (*Atriplex lentiformis*). All zones. Large, unevenly rounded shrub growing to 5 to 10 feet and spreading 6 to 12 feet. Densely branched with twigs spreading and angled. Leaves are bluish-gray. Twigs, gray to white. Becomes deciduous early in dry soil; almost evergreen with moisture.

Four-wing salt bush, or **chamiso** (*A. canescens*). Dense growth of brittle twigs to 3 to 6 feet high and spreading 4 to 8 feet. Small leaves are densely coated gray above and below. Good in mass plantings as a hillside cover. Can be trimmed as a hedge.

Desert honeysuckle (*Anisacanthus thurberi*). Adapted as perennial in zones 10 and 11. Taller growing with stout branches in zones 12 and 13. A deciduous shrub that is best treated as a perennial and cut to the ground each winter. Will grow to about 3 feet by June when it starts its summer display of orange-red tubular flowers held above its light-green foliage. Effective when massed. Combines attractively with Texas ranger.

Chuparosa (*Beloperone californica*). Zones 10, 11, 12, 13. Leaves are so small that the arching, gray-green, velvety-haired branches appear almost leafless. Grows from 2 to 5 feet. Valued for its clusters of tubular, bright-red flowers in April and May.

Multistemmed, wide-spreading sweet acacia ideal for filtered shade. Heaviest bloom January to May.

Desert ironwood (*Olneya tesota*). Zones 12, 13. Evergreen in mild winters. Shrub-tree, slow-growing to 5 to 15 feet. Handsome lavender flowers in May and June.

Honey mesquite (*Prosopis glandulosa torreyana*). All zones. Evergreen or semi-evergreen large shrub or tree to 30 feet high and 40 feet wide depending upon water supply.

Screw bean mesquite (*P. pubescens*). All zones. More spiny than the honey mesquite. Gets its name from its coiled seed pod.

Outstanding in drought resistance but responds to deep watering. Interesting when planted in groves and the trees high-pruned. Useful in tough situations as a high screen or windbreak.

Desert elderberry (*Sambucus mexicana*). All zones. A large deciduous shrub or tree to 30 feet or more. Similar to the blue elderberry, but with fewer and smaller leaflets, small drier berries.

Ocotillo forms cluster of whip-like thorny stems. Brilliant red flowers top stems April to June.

Yellow trumpet flower with shining yellow-green leaves is used effectively at entryway in Indio.

Fairy duster, or **false mesquite** (*Calliandra eriophylla*). Zones 10, 11, 12, 13. A low bushy shrub of gray twigs making a wide open mound to 3 feet. Grown for its interesting flower clusters with pink to red stamens in fluffy balls, in February or March.

Cassia (*Cassia wislizenii*). Zones 10, 11, 12, 13. Commonly grown in gardens around Bisbee, Arizona. Native to Arizona, New Mexico, and Texas. Deciduous shrub to 4 to 9 feet. Many-branched with dark bark. Large yellow flowers in June through September.

Brittlebush or **incienso** (*Encelia farinosa*). Zones 10, 11, 12, 13. Low-branching, deciduous shrub to about 3 feet. Small gray-green leaves. Calls attention to itself in spring with orange-yellow flowers on long naked branchlets.

Apache plume (*Fallugia paradoxa*). Zones 10, 11, 12, 13. A deciduous shrub of rather rigid pattern of small, straw-colored branches. Grows slowly to about 5 feet. White flowers in April and May are followed with lavender, feathery fruits that are the "plumes" of the plant.

Ocotillo (*Fouquieria splendens*). Deciduous shrub made up by many whiplike spiny stems 8 to 15 feet high. Leaves appear after rains, soon drop. Tubular red flowers in clusters atop the many stems create a striking display. Keep it under drought conditions, water infrequently to bring into bloom.

Creosote bush (*Larrea divaricata*). Zones 10, 11, 12, 13. Probably the commonest shrub in the deserts. Many upright branches 4 to 8 feet tall. Small varnished leaves. Responds to water and fertilizer with larger, shiny, dark-green leaves. Use as wind or privacy screen, or trim into a hedge.

Lysiloma (*Lysiloma microphylla*). Zones 12, 13. Large deciduous shrub to 9 feet with feathery, canopied foliage. White flowers in May and June.

Feathery cassia boundary screen is on edge of, not in, dichondra lawn.

Sugar bush (*Rhus ovata*). Zones 10, 11, 12, 13. Winter damage at 10°. Evergreen shrub to 15 feet and as wide. Bright green, leathery leaves. Cream-colored flowers (red buds) in March to May.

Jojoba (in Arizona), **goatnut** (in California), also called **coffee-bush, quinine plant** (*Simmondsia chinensis*). Zones 10, 11, 12, 13. Evergreen shrub from 3 to 6 feet with thick, leathery leaves and edible fruits that resemble small acorns.

Yellow trumpet flower, yellow bells (*Stenolobium stans*, formerly *Tecoma stans*). Zones 12, 13. Growth habit depends on where you find it. It's low-growing and deciduous in the cold-winter areas of its range. It's a 3 to 6-foot deciduous shrub in Tucson. And it's a large 12 to 20-foot evergreen shrub that can be trained as a small tree in Brawley and Needles. Spectacular with its bright yellow, trumpet-shaped flowers and bright green foliage in August and September.

SUCCULENTS AND CACTUS

The biggest, boldest succulents and cactus seem to shout "This is the desert". Yucca, agave, saguaro, organpipe cactus, tree cereus, opuntia—these are plants for people who want a garden that matches the mood of the wild desert. And they're for people who want a garden that almost takes care of itself.

Also important to desert gardeners are the succulents and cactus that aren't big and bold. The little ones have earned a place in a desert home landscape—as pattern plants, in rock gardens, in garden situations where you can see them up close. But they're grown most often by hobbyists who gather, pamper, study, and cherish them like a stamp collection. Collectors treasure them for their great variety of shapes and sizes, for their colorful flowers, and for their oddness.

Realize that here we're talking about two tremendous categories of plants. Strictly speaking, the term succulent refers to any plant that stores water in juicy leaves, stems, or roots in order to withstand periodic drought. There are thousands of succulents, and they exist throughout the plant world. For instance, there are succulents in the lily family, the daisy family, and the cactus family. All members of the cactus family are succulents, but cactus are so special that they deserve to be singled out.

All cactus (except possibly one) are native to the Western Hemisphere. They grow wild from Canada to Argentina, from below sea level to over three miles high. Some grow in dripping jungles, while others grow in arid deserts. The Southwest desert, of course, is the most famous of all the cactus lands for seeing native cactus in the wild and for growing natives and exotics in the garden.

Generally, cactus have no leaves. They have stems modified into cylinders, pads, or joints that store precious water during drought. Thick skin reduces evaporation. Most of them have spines. Flowers usually are large and bright. Sometimes they're brilliant, really fantastic, otherworldly—as you know if you've ever seen the desert in bloom with fishhook cactus, barrel cactus, cholla, hedgehog cactus, and pincushion cactus.

Landscaping with succulents and cactus

Figure that the bigger ones are pieces of garden sculpture and place them accordingly. Give them an open, prominent spot. Show them off against a stucco or brick background. Keep them company with a boulder or two. A gravel mulch underneath looks neat, keeps weeds down, and fills out the stark, dramatic setting.

Make the landscape scheme simple. Try to avoid the splotchy effect that comes with a random assortment of many different kinds. Instead stick with large groups of a single kind.

The smaller plants are most practical in containers. There you can give them the sort of care they need (described below), protect them from frost, and see them better. Most of the large cactus take several years before they're big enough to show up in the garden. While you're waiting for them to grow up, keep containers displayed on the patio or another prominent spot.

Usually a plain, one-colored pot sets off a plant best. As a rule, use a container that looks a little on the small side. Use a pot an inch or so wider than the diameter of the plant; or crowd lots of plants into a single pot.

OWNER-ARCHITECT: JACK CATLIN

Succulents in containers are pleasant garden features. Here echeveria in shallow soy tub.

Bold structural forms of columnar cereus, evergreen magnolia, and yucca with swordlike leaves frame wooden carvings at entrance to adobe brick home.

Small succulents hardy enough to spend the winters outdoors make good small-scale ground covers —if you're willing to give them careful attention. These include hen and chicks (*Echeveria* and *Sempervivum*), red spike ice plant (*Cephalophyllum* 'Red Spike', often sold as *Cylindrophyllum speciosum*), and croceum ice plant (*Malephora crocea,* often sold as *Hymenocyclus*). Many of the sedums look good, but they have shallow roots and need frequent watering. They're often used as ground covers.

Or try spotting hen and chicks and other little succulents in casual, natural-looking situations—in a crack in stone or paving, between flagstone steps, tucked into a stone wall.

Cactus—A baker's dozen

Saguaro (*Carnegiea gigantea*). Zones 12 and 13. Native to northern Mexico, Arizona, and California. The characteristic plant of Arizona and Sonora. Columnar and branching with prominent ribs that give it a fluted appearance. So slow growing that a plant stays pot or garden-sized for years. Big white blossom is Arizona's state flower.

Organpipe cactus (*Lemaireocereus thurberi*). Zones 12 and 13. Native to Arizona and Mexico. Big, columnar treelike cactus that usually branches from the bottom (branches from top if plant is injured). Dark green to grayish. Slow growing to 15 feet. Night-blooming flowers, purplish with white edges.

Barrel cactus (*Echinocactus*). Hardiness depends on origin. The California, or compass, barrel (*E. acanthodes*) is native to southwest Arizona as well as the mountains of the Mojave Desert up to 3,500 feet. It has great stout stems, 2 to 3 feet long (sometimes 5 feet or more). They're armed with straight spines varying in color from bright red to yellow.

Coville barrel cactus (*E. covillei*). Native to Arizona and Sonora, Mexico, at elevations of 1,500 to 3,000 feet. Roundish cactus 2 to 8 feet high, 1 to 2 feet in diameter. Larger plants are tall, cylindrical—among the most distinctive of all the barrel cactus. Spines curve backwards so you can pick up a plant without getting stuck.

Cotton-top (*E. polycephalus*). Native to Mojave Desert, California, Arizona, northern Sonora, southern Utah. Low growing in clumps. Roundish heads 8 to 10 inches in diameter. Yellow flowers in a crowning circle. Dry fruits are very woolly with white matted hairs.

Fishhook barrel cactus (*Ferocactus wislizenii*). Widely distributed in Arizona, Sonora, and to the western tip of Texas, 1,200 to 5,000 feet elevation. Columnar cactus 2 to 8 feet high, 1 to 2 feet in diameter. Roundish when growing tip has been destroyed. Central spines strongly hooked.

Clump of polka-dots (Opuntia microdasys albispina) *starts to trail over wall.*

Opuntia. This big group includes two types of cactus: the prickly pears, with flat, broad joints; and the chollas, with cylindrical joints.

Indian fig cactus (*Opuntia ficus-indica*). Zones 12 and 13. One of the largest of the prickly pears. Shrubby or treelike up to 15 feet. Large pads up to 2 feet long. Few or no spines, but clusters of bristles. Yellow flowers 4 inches across. Large, edible yellow or red fruit often sold in markets.

Pancake pear (*O. chlorotica*). Native from southeastern California to southwestern Utah, mostly on rocky, sunny ledges, at elevations of 2,500 to 6,000 feet. Shrub or small tree, 3 to 6 feet high, several feet thick. Branches have many joints—usually five to ten. Joints are like pancakes, almost round, flat, 6 to 8 inches long, 5 to 7 inches broad.

Beaver-tail cactus (*O. basilaris*). Native from California to Arizona to southern Utah between elevations of 200 to 3,000 feet. A low-growing prickly pear, usually between 6 and 12 inches tall. Joints are roundish, flat, smooth looking.

Purple prickly pear (*O. gosseliniana santa-rita*). Native to Arizona. Short-trunked treelike cactus, 2 to 5 feet high. Roundish, spineless joints, about 6 inches wide. Young plants turn purple with cold. Older ones usually remain purple all year.

Teddybear cactus (*O. bigelovii*). Native to Colorado and elevations of 90 to 3,000 feet in Arizona. One of the most striking of all the chollas. Stocky and treelike, 2 to 5 feet tall. Short branches at or near top of column. Spines probably the most vicious of all cactus.

Bunny ears (*O. microdasys*). Cholla native to northern Mexico. Clumping, bushy cactus that spreads wider (4 to 5 feet) than it grows tall (about 2 feet). Pads are flat and thin, nearly round, up to 6 inches across, velvety, soft green.

Distinctive Yucca recurvifolia *with sword-shaped leaves, clusters of white flowers, is popular.*

DESIGN: LOUIS D. GERLACH

Dramatic Yucca thompsoniana *among lava rock dominates this planting group.*

The yuccas—bold and basic

Spanish bayonet, or **aloe yucca** (*Yucca aloifolia*). Slow growing to 10 feet or more, generally as a straight single stem densely clothed from the ground up with sharply pointed leaves from 1 to 2 feet long. Trunks sometimes sprawl to give a picturesque effect. The variegated form is most attractive. Hardy all zones.

Banana yucca, or **dactil yucca** (*Y. baccata*). Multiple trunks at different heights, swollen at the base. Blue-green, 2-foot-long leaves with coarse fibers along margins. Flowers are fleshy, red-brown outside, white inside, and are carried in a dense cluster above the foliage. Hardy all zones.

Joshua tree (*Y. brevifolia*). This tree yucca with its grotesque branches ranks with the saguaro, or giant cactus, as a symbol of the desert. It is the distinctive plant of the Mojave Desert, just as the saguaro symbolizes the Sonoran Desert in Arizona. Age old trees will reach 30 feet or more in height with trunks from 2 to 4 feet in diameter. Nursery plants are very slow to make trunks. Moving plants from the desert is seldom successful even when done by professionals.

Soap-tree yucca, or **palmilla** (*Y. elata*). A stemless rosette of leaves when young, it develops into a tree form to 6 feet or more with single or branched trunk. Flowers are carried 3 to 6 feet above long, narrow, gray-green leaves. One of the most common yuccas in northern Arizona, New Mexico, Texas.

Giant yucca (*Y. elephantipes,* often sold as *Y. gigantea*). A large tree yucca with picturesque trunks, each topped with a rosette of thick green leaves up to 4 feet long. A native of Mexico, it is tender to frost and is reported to freeze at 22°. However, its landscape value as a dramatic accent plant has encouraged plantings in zones 12 and 13.

Adam's needle (*Y. filamentosa*). Bold rosettes of blue-green leaves with numerous long loose fibers along their edges. The flowering stem reaches to a height of 7 feet or more and carries showy white flowers in loose branching clusters. Hardy all zones.

Great plains yucca (*Y. glauca*). Narrow (½-inch) leaves, 2 feet long, in a stemless rosette. Fine textured foliage combines well with agave and coarser-leafed yucca. Flowers on 6-foot stalks are greenish white. Hardy all zones.

Curve leaf yucca (*Y. recurvifolia,* often sold as *Y. pendula*). A tree yucca that grows as a single trunk, branching in age, to 6 feet or more. Branches bear several foliage heads, each producing rather open clusters of white flowers. Beautiful gray-blue-green leaves 2 to 3 feet long and 2 inches wide, bend sharply downward. One of the best for landscape use. Combines well with blue agaves. Hardy all zones except cold areas of 10X.

Our Lord's candle (*Y. whipplei*). Native to Southern California mountains, California coast, Baja California. Stemless rosettes of gray-green leaves 1 to 2 feet long. Leaves are needle sharp; don't plant where people can walk into them. Flowering stems 6 to 14 feet long carry large spikes of creamy white flowers. Plants die after blooming. New plants come from seeds or offsets. Its blooming is a dramatic event. Speed of growth is unbelievable. In less than 30 days after the stem emerges it shoots up to 10 feet or more with its white bells in full display around the top 4 feet of the stem.

A native plant that is sometimes mistaken for *Y. whipplei* is the Parry nolina. The flower cluster is dramatic, but the individual flowers are smaller and the cluster very dense and compact. Leaves are more grasslike. Another nolina, commonly called bear grass (*Nolina microcarpa*) growing to less than 3 feet, is very showy when in flower.

Bold century plants Agave americana add dramatic effect to neat garden in Paradise Valley, Arizona.

Donkey tail sedum in stand would make decorative display in any desert garden.

The yuccas, like the agaves, will tolerate much drier conditions than most other leaf succulents, but they will accept and thrive on normal garden watering. When planting yucca or agave from nursery cans, build a basin around the plant and fill basin with water every 4 to 5 days until it is in good growing condition.

The versatile agave

In the Southwest desert you can see nine different kinds of agave growing wild—only a few of a huge group of more than 250 species native to tropical and subtropical America. They range in size from monsters like the century plant to some no bigger than a head of lettuce. The wild ones are protected by law and can't be collected. But you can quite easily obtain and grow the century plant (*Agave americana*) in zones 12 and 13.

The century plant is a big, bulky succulent with 6-foot leaves that have spines all along the edges and one at the tip. It doesn't take 100 years to bloom—but more like 10. The flower stalk reaches up 15 to 40 feet. After blooming, the clump dies.

Taking care of succulents

Most gardeners expect something for nothing from succulents. While it's true that many endure neglect, almost all look better if given careful attention. Remember that not all succulents are natives of hot, dry places.

First of all, start with soil that drains quickly. If your soil doesn't, plant in raised beds or containers. You can fill the raised beds and containers with a prepared, lightweight, porous soil mixture; or you can mix your own. Here's a good mix for most succulents: equal parts of good topsoil, coarse sand, and either leaf mold, ground bark, or peat moss.

Almost all of the little succulents need shade in the early afternoon. Echeveria and sedum are two of the few exceptions that can take sun during the hot part of the day.

As a general rule, most succulents in pots or in the ground need water once or twice a week during the active growing season. (Many times in late spring and summer, even daily watering isn't too often.) Here's another general rule: Water as soon as the soil surface dries out. That means occasional watering during the winter—about once every two or three weeks.

Agaves and yuccas ignore the normal watering rules. They get along very well when watered as frequently as recommended above, but they can do with less. After planting them from nursery cans, build a basin around the plant and fill it with water every four or five days until new growth gets well underway. After that, water whenever they seem to need it.

Lift and divide succulents when they become crowded. Fast-growing kinds need going over every two or three years. Replant only the largest and strongest divisions.

When stems of taller succulents, such as some echeverias, get too long, cut them off about an inch below each rosette, and replant these short-stemmed pieces. (Ideally, of course, you would place these cut-off rosettes in a box or flat of sand, and plant them out after they have formed strong roots.)

Taking care of cactus

Cactus need less water and special care than the general run of succulents. Still they respond quite noticeably to good gardening.

Almost all cactus need a warm, full sun location. When it comes to soil, cactus need pretty much the same thing as succulents—good, fast drainage (if anything, faster than for succulents). Roots rot easily if they're growing in poorly drained soil. As said above for succulents, if your soil doesn't drain quickly, plant in raised beds or containers. Use a lightweight, porous planting mix such as the one suggested for succulents.

After transplanting cactus to the garden, don't water for several days. Thereafter, water sparingly— once every four to six weeks—until the root system becomes established.

When they are established, cactus require water in order to reach their potential in size and bloom. Water thoroughly, then let soil dry out before you water again. During the period of active spring growth, water as often as every 7 to 10 days. In fall and winter, cactus need less water. In fact, at this time they should be allowed to go dormant; excessive watering might encourage tender new growth that would be easily damaged by a frost.

Cactus require large amounts of food to produce good growth and an abundance of flowers and fruit. From April through September, feed once a month with a complete, liquid-type fertilizer.

Although cactus look rugged, aphids, mealybug, red spider mites, thrips, and scale sometimes attack them. When necessary, spray with a multipurpose insecticide. Cactus are sensitive to many insecticides, so use caution when applying them to your plants. Spray only when the sun is not shining directly on plants, preferably early morning or late evening.

Some cactus are quite tender to frost. If the plants go dormant as cold weather approaches, they will have greater resistance. You can encourage dormancy by withholding nitrogen fertilizer and cutting down on the watering schedule during the fall and winter months. Also, you can cover the tip growth of frost-tender plants with burlap, a clear plastic refrigerator bag, or similar material.

Growing succulents from cuttings

Many of the choicest succulents for sale at nurseries are quite expensive if you buy large plants. Fortunately it isn't difficult to increase your supply, once you have a good plant, just by taking leaf cuttings.

Cuttings of succulents usually root best during the warmth of spring and summer. If you have a heated propagating bed, you can root them any time of year.

It isn't necessary to start with a perfect leaf. Often one that has been sunburned or disfigured in some other way will work just as well. But avoid leaves that are rotted or diseased.

For rooting cuttings and growing them to flowering-sized plants, use a mix of two parts coarse river sand, one part finely screened peat moss, and one part leaf mold (or use clean, coarse sand by itself). Lay cuttings out in the air for a day or two before

potting them, to dry out the cut ends and discourage rot. After planting, water sparingly. Cuttings in a 5 or 6-inch clay pan probably won't require watering more than twice a week. Never water before the surface of the soil dries out. After October 1 reduce watering to a minimum. Too much soil moisture tends to encourage rot.

Transplanting cactus

Desert gardeners often find it necessary to move a cactus plant from one garden location to another. Since these plants build up a thick layer of protective tissue on the south and southwest side, it is important to keep the more tender, north-facing tissue from being exposed to the full intensity of the sun. Before transplanting, mark the north side with chalk or a plant tie, and replant in the same relative position.

With a sharp shovel, dig a 6-inch-deep trench about 6 to 12 inches away from the plant—depending on the size of the cactus—and lift or pry out of the ground. Remove soil from the roots and dust with sulfur. Move to a shady location with good air circulation for about a week before replanting. This allows bruised roots to heal.

Plant in dry soil, and stake if necessary. Do not water the plant until new growth starts— usually in about three or four weeks. Afterwards water once every four to six weeks until the root system becomes established. For rapid growth, water with a transplanting hormone the first and second irrigations.

Big Joshua tree (Yucca brevifolia) *is the dominating feature of this California garden.*

SPECIALTIES: PALMS, CYCADS, AND CITRUS

Desert garden specialties like the palm, the cycad, and the citrus offer great opportunities for imaginative landscape planning. With so many varieties adapted to the desert, particularly of the palm tree (which we discuss the most here), there is no limit to the uses of these plants in the garden design. They are effective standing alone, combined with other plants, growing in containers, positioned at entries.

Versatile and adaptive, these specialties will add height or fullness; quiet, pleasing shapes or exclamation points to your landscape—always capturing interest. No matter which position you select for them to fill, they will be distinctive features of your garden and will give you much pleasure for many years.

Palms

Today we think of the palm in terms of its decorative function. In the ancient history of gardening, it held even loftier positions. To the Assyrians the ultimate symbol of eternal life was a tree growing beside a stream. The tree above all others to them was the palm. The earliest Assyrian gardens were probably nothing more than a grove of date palms near the house. No tree at that time was so generous in its service to man; the palm provided building materials and necessary parts of the national diet. Vegetables, exotic trees and shrubs, and fragrant flowers were introduced only later.

Any plant family as large, ancient, and cosmopolitan as the palm is bound to have a member adapted to any garden situation. And as with any large family (the palm has some 3,000 species), it is both easy and misleading to judge all the members by the characteristics of just a known few. An acquaintance with the types of palms available in the desert today will let you know what each of them can do for a garden, patio, or interior.

The distinctive tree

Palms appear most strikingly as the tall unbranched trunk that we see curved in Hawaii but grown straight in California as the native washingtonia pictured on the facing page. Palms also grow in modest size with an unbranched trunk, in bamboo-like thickets (miniature or giant), as clumps with curving offshoots, even as vines.

Second to its trunk, a palm's most distinctive characteristic is its leaf. Palms grow naturally by their leaves; they are either fans or feathers. The trees shown on this and the opposite page are fan palms. The date palm on page 58 is an example of a feather palm.

In nature, palms grow in solid stands, but also liberally mixed with other plants, usually broad-leafed evergreen trees and shrubs. They often grow under high spreading trees in youth, and grow above the forest only in maturity.

Lacy fronds of Dioon edule *appear etched against large rock and trunk of California fan palm.*

Trio of California palms in Palm Springs dominate their surroundings. A use like this intentionally subordinates everything else.

Date palms above contrast in form with fan palms across Palm Springs street. Right, *severely pruned, they shade house where they were once part of grove.*

Palm trees at home

One of the trademarks of Palm Springs, and also of Indio, Yuma, Phoenix, and other low desert communities, is a skyline punctuated with the distinctive silhouette of palm trees.

In the low desert, two tall species dominate: the California fan palm (*Washingtonia filifera*), a native of the oases and foothill canyons near Palm Springs, and the Mexican fan palm (*W. robusta*).

The California fan palm is distinguished from the Mexican fan palm in several ways. The most immediately apparent difference is in its trunk, which is two or three times as thick as that of the Mexican palm. The California fan palm grows to 70 or 80 feet. Its dull green leaves, 6 feet long and 5 feet wide, droop at the ends of segments, each of which has many threadlike fibers.

The Mexican fan palm has sparkling green leaves that are not as long or as wide; the ends of the segments do not droop, and the mature leaves lack the characteristic fibers of the California fan palm. The leaf crown looks more compact than that of the California palm. The tall, slender trunk is swollen at the base. Trees reach 65 to 70 feet in height.

Other palms grown in low desert communities include: another tall species, the date palm (*Phoenix dactylifera*), a favorite along streets and for golf courses; the European fan palm (*Chamaerops humilis*), 10 to 20 feet high with a 25-foot spread; Senegal date palm (*Phoenix reclinata*), 15 to 25 feet, with a leaning trunk; pigmy date palm (*Phoenix roebelenii*), slow-growing to 4 to 8 feet, with a 3 to 6-foot spread; pindo palm (*Butia capitata*, usually sold as *Cocos australis*), 10 to 20 feet high, with a 10 to 15-foot spread; and the Mexican blue palm (*Erythea armata*), slow-growing to 15 or sometimes 30 feet, with a 10 or 12-foot spread.

In the high desert, the winters are too cold for most palms, but the following have been grown: the California fan palm, which may need winter protection for its first few years here; and the Mexican fan palm, which is much like it, but hardier in this zone.

Some small to medium-sized palms for areas of occasional frost are: *Acrocomia totai*, butia, *Chamaedorea elegans*, *C. klotzschiana*, *C. seifrizii*, livistonas, rhapidophyllum, trachycarpus.

The palm plays many parts

With their varied characteristics, palm trees rise to many occasions. Here are some of the roles that the right kinds of palms can fill:

Sturdy palms for park and avenue plantings, and for vertical effects in large gardens: erytheas, livistonas, *Phoenix canariensis*, *P. dactylifera*, *P. humilis*, sabals, washingtonias.

Palms near swimming pools: Palms have great value near swimming pools because they do not drop leaves. Mature plants of *Chamaerops humilis*, with their curved trunks arching near the pool, give a feeling of a tropical island. But whether palm trunks are curved or upright, or topped with either fan or feather leaves, they create beautiful mirror effects in the water.

Palms to light at night: Because of their stateliness and their spectacular leaves, palms are good subjects for night lighting. You can back-light them, light them from below, or direct lights to silhouette palms against a light-colored building wall.

Palms as ground covers: Young palms, especially those that grow slowly such as *Livistona chinensis* or *Chamaerops humilis*, can be used effectively as ground covers. They'll stay low for from 5 to 10 years, especially if they're in gardens that need little care. When they get too tall, move them to another location in the garden where you need height.

Compare skirts of wild California fan palms above with slender, smooth trunks of Mexican fan palms to right with skirts, leaf bases removed.

Plant palms in the summer

Summer is the time to plant palms, since they need heat in order to establish strong root systems. Desert nurseries, many of which carry unusual kinds, have a good supply on hand during the summer months. In selecting a palm, consider eventual size as well as ornamental appeal and climate adaptability. The Mexican blue palm (*Erythea armata*) is one of the most desirable on all three counts.

Although established palm trees survive and even manage to grow in poor, dry soil, they will grow much faster and look better in fertile soil. When you prepare the planting hole, mix a liberal amount of peat moss, ground bark, or other organic material with the excavated soil to use as backfill. Make the hole 3 feet wide (for a 5-gallon, container-grown palm) and 8 inches deeper than the root ball or container. At the bottom of the hole add 1 or 2 cubic feet of steer manure and mix in some blood meal. Cover this with a 6-inch layer of backfill soil.

Set in the palm tree, fill in the hole with backfill soil, and soak well. Pull up earth to make a watering basin, and continue to water until fall rains begin. Note the drawing on this page.

If you are transplanting a palm, you needn't take a large root ball. New roots will develop in a short time to replace those lost in digging, Be sure to anchor the plant firmly in place with stakes and guy wires. Some gardeners tie up the outer fronds of newly planted palms to protect tender center buds until they have developed sufficiently to escape damage from extreme heat or drying winds.

Nurseries will supply slow and fast-growing palms in containers like these.

Palm trees need little care

Palms demand less maintenance than most trees. Reasonably fertile soil and adequate watering—even for the native desert kinds—will produce thriving plants; most palms used in California and Arizona thrive on astonishingly little care.

Washing down palms with a hose is very beneficial, especially to those trees exposed to dust and beyond the reach of rain or dew. Frequent washing will provide some humidity and dislodge insects such as scale, mites, and mealybugs that find refuge in the long-leafed stems of some varieties.

Feather palms and many fan palms look neater when old leaves are removed after they have turned brown. Make neat cuts close to the trunk, leaving the leaf bases. Some palms shed the old leaf bases on their own. Others, including arecastrums and chamaedoreas, may hold the old bases. You can remove them by making shallow slices next to the trunk.

Many palm admirers say that the dead leaves of washingtonias should remain on the tree, the thatch being part of the palm's character. See the photograph on page 59. If you also feel this way, you can cut lower fronds in a uniform way close to the trunk, but leave the leaf bases which present a rather pleasant lattice surface.

Most young palms prefer shade; all tolerate it. This is what makes them such good house or patio plants at a stage when they are house or patio size. As they grow, they can be moved into full sun or part shade, depending on the species.

Growth rate varies considerably among palms, but keeping the plants in pots will in most cases slow down the growth of those which have a tendency to take off. When temperatures are above the 60's, fertilize your potted palms often and wash them off frequently to provide some humidity. The washing will also dislodge insects.

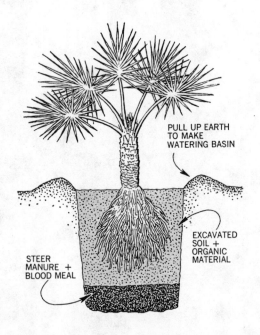

PULL UP EARTH
TO MAKE
WATERING BASIN

EXCAVATED
SOIL +
ORGANIC
MATERIAL

STEER
MANURE +
BLOOD MEAL

Organic material in soil and plant food at bottom of hole get palm off to a fast start.

Cycads

Cycads are popular features in desert gardens. Around Palm Springs, California, cycads stand out as stellar performers, looking proud, clean, and healthy. They are rich and exotic in character, usable in many different ways, and always impressive. In their youth, cycads have an airy, lacy quality reminiscent of ferns. As they get older (they grow *very* slowly), these plants look more like palms than ferns (the most widely grown species, *Cycas revoluta*, is commonly called the sago palm). But cycads are neither ferns nor palms—they are primitive, cone-bearing plants related to (but antedating) conifers.

Although cycads are natives of moist tropical areas, they are remarkably adapted to desert climates, if protected from hottest sun and wind, and if the soil is kept moist (never soggy).

The sago palm is the hardiest and most adaptable of all cycads now in cultivation. The young plants have single trunks; multiple branching occurs only after many years. Mature height is 6 to 10 feet. Young leaves are blue-green, later turning dark green. Most sago palms grow in enclosed or partially enclosed areas on the east or north sides of houses or walls, where they receive morning and afternoon shade. On the other hand, to illustrate how well this plant can adjust to various conditions, it has been known to thrive in an open exposure where it received full sun almost all day. The important thing is never to place a cycad directly against a wall that reflects direct heat.

LANDSCAPE ARCHITECT: WARREN JONES

Handsome sago palm is center of interest at entry with Asparagus sprengeri, *evergreen grape vine.*

Dioon in covered entry garden on west side of house receives strong light but no direct sun.

Picturesque, 20-year-old dwarf sago palm growing in bonsai container is displayed on low bench.

Another cycad, more tender and less frequently sold, is the *Dioon edule* seen in the picture on the preceding page. It is especially interesting because it is closer to fossil forms than any of the other cycads now living. This plant, native to the east coast of Mexico, eventually forms a cylindrical trunk 6 to 10 inches in diameter and 3 feet tall; its leaves are 3 to 5 feet long.

Leaves on young plants of *D. edule* are a beautiful shade of dusty blue-green, and are soft and feathery in texture. On mature plants, leaves are dark green above, lighter beneath, and are more rigid, with a hard, shiny texture.

Care for cycads

Although cycads are not temperamental about soil, they respond favorably to a growing medium with at least 30 per cent organic matter (leaf mold, peat moss, or ground bark) and invariably require fast drainage. Where natural drainage is adequate, grow cycads in raised beds or in containers. A yearly application of complete fertilizer, just as the plant is starting to put out new growth, is recommended by some specialists.

Sago palm with several trunks makes splendid feature in raised bed entry to Palm Springs home.

Citrus for the desert

Citrus trees and shrubs are much in demand as fruit and landscape plants. They offer attractive form and foliage all year, fragrant flowers out of season, and decorative fruit in season.

Citrus trees in the landscape

As producers of quality fruit, varieties must be selected according to two considerations: total amount of heat available through the fruit-developing period (need varies according to type), and the winter cold they will get. Choice and use are also determined by whether plants are standard trees or dwarfs.

Standard or dwarf. Most standard citrus trees grow to 20 to 30 feet high and almost as wide. Dwarfs (grown on dwarfing stock) become 4 to 10-foot shrubs or small trees of equal beauty and greater landscaping utility. They can be located more easily than standards in garden warm spots and in containers where they can be protected easily from frost and placed in wind-protected warm spots for extra heat.

Citrus look forlorn when neglected, luxuriant when well trained. Actually, their culture is no more exacting than for roses, camellias, and azaleas.

Espalier. Almost all citrus can be trained to grow as an informal or formal espalier. They are trained on wire or frame at least 6 inches from fence or wall. Keep bending branches to grow horizontally. Pinch back new growth that takes off in the wrong direction.

Hedges. One ideal plant for hedge use is shown on this page and the next. It is the compact-growing

'Bouquet' sour orange has dark green foliage and decorative bright orange fruits.

'Bouquet' sour orange, often called 'Bouquet des Fleurs,' that grows well in the Tucson and Phoenix areas. Several planted as a hedge can be kept to 8 or 10 feet by pruning. Let a single plant grow naturally, and it will become a 12 to 15-foot-high tree.

Citrus in containers. Daily watering may be necessary in hot weather. For most dwarf citrus, containers should be at least 18 inches in diameter. In the picture below, a dwarf Eustis limequat is set in a container in a mixture of half topsoil, half peat, and mulched with gravel. It will bear fruit year-around in mild climate areas.

Natural hardiness and care the gardener must give

Citrus of one kind or another are grown in every Arizona and California climate where winter temperatures do not fall below 20°. From least hardy to hardiest they rank generally in this order: 'Mexican' lime (28°), limequat, grapefruit, regular lemon, tangelo and tangor, 'Bearss' lime, sweet orange, most mandarin oranges (tangerines), 'Rangpur' lime and 'Meyer' lemon, 'Owari' mandarin, sour orange, kumquat, calamondin (20°).

A navel orange tree needs heat and has a short developing period so would be a good choice for Arizona areas. Mandarin oranges (tangerine group) and grapefruit also need much heat for top flavor.

Drainage. The first requirement is fast drainage. If soil drains slowly, don't attempt to plant citrus in it regardless of how you condition planting soil. In poorly drained soil, plant above soil level in raised beds or by mounding up soil around the plant. Drainage in average soil and water retention in very light soils will be improved by digging in a 4 to 6-inch layer of peat moss, sawdust, or ground bark to a depth of 12 inches.

Watering. Citrus needs moist soil, but never free-standing water. It needs air in the soil. Danger from overwatering is greatest in clay soil where air spaces are minute. In soil with proper drainage, water newly planted trees almost as frequently as trees in containers—twice a week in normal summer weather, more frequently during a hot spell. Water established trees every other week. In clay soils, space watering intervals so top part of soil dries between irrigations. Don't let tree reach wilting point (as has often been advised in the past).

If you build basins, make them wider than the spread of branches. Citrus roots extend out twice as far as the distance from the trunk to branch ends. Keep trunk dry by starting basin 6 inches or more from trunk. When you water, put on enough to wet the entire root zone (that is, wet to a depth of 4 feet). Notice the citrus trees growing by the pool in the picture on this page. Each has a large basin out to the drip line for watering and mulching.

Orange hedge makes an attractive, dense, 12-foot-high screen along Phoenix drive.

Dwarf Eustis limequat looks good in container, bears fruit year-around in mild-winter areas.

Citrus trees in Palm Springs garden have basins out to drip line for deep watering, mulching.

SEASONAL FLOWERS AND VEGETABLES

We recognize flowers as landscape materials of a very special nature: as plants to delight the gardener who enjoys color and finds no end of satisfaction in working out different combinations of colors; and as practical, easy problem-solvers in situations found in many gardens.

Vegetables, of course, are old favorites, whose cultivation brings an enjoyment and satisfaction all its own. You'll see later in this chapter that your vegetable plantings can yield a visually rewarding crop as well as an edible one.

Flowers for all seasons

The trend toward low maintenance gardens with all their paving, gravel, or ground covers doesn't eliminate the need for flowers. In fact, the garden largely given over to paving and structure often needs their color most, and its very design frequently lends itself to some dramatic displays of concentrated color. The raised bed is an ideal staging area, and so are the many pockets left under trees or around a paved patio. And, of course, you can also grow flowers in pots or in some of the interesting ceramic, concrete, wood, and other kinds of containers now available. It's only a matter of choosing those that are in proper scale, and adapted to the exposure.

Among the most reliable perennials for desert areas are chrysanthemums. If you keep the plants compact and growing vigorously during the spring and summer months, they will give you a colorful show of blooms in the fall.

Chrysanthemums grow most vigorously in May and June; therefore, they'll need lots of water. Water in furrows or use soil soakers.

There is no special way you must plant bulbs in the desert. Follow the same directions as outlined in the *Sunset* book, *How to Grow Bulbs,* and the *Sunset Western Garden Book.*

Annuals

Annuals bring maximum color to a garden in minimum time—in every color imaginable. Most of them are inexpensive. They come in all shapes and sizes. No plants are easier to grow. They provide an element of fun and a sense of discovery for any gardener—from the fumbling beginner to the experienced plantsman.

Annuals are especially effective as problem-solvers. Spot a few here and there as fillers in bare spots and corners, between young shrubs, or among perennials. Try them as edgings, background plantings, or bulb covers. If you have the space and the proper situation, mass them in one or two locations.

Perhaps the most noteworthy quality of annuals is their ability to grow in a hurry; they are the speed merchants of the gardening world.

In a new garden, they provide a carnival of color, and at the same time fill in barren areas between young shrubs and trees that are not yet the large, dominating forms they'll be several years from now. Above all, let this be your rule: Put them where you can see them and enjoy their color to the fullest.

During prime planting time in October, nurseries feature wide selection of chrysanthemums.

Madagascar periwinkle with showy rose pink flowers in summer and fall, grows under palm tree in neat planting bed border of patio in Phoenix garden.

DESIGN: ALLEN GUARD

In October, gardener planted mixed border along south-facing wall—stock, petunias, sweet alyssum.

In April, she had pleasant, old-fashioned mixture of spikes, clumps in many colors, mixed fragrances.

Fall is spring in the low desert

The best planting season of the year for low desert Arizonans and Californians starts in September and continues through October and into November. You have then the very best opportunity of the year to plant the classic, flower-laden spring and summer flower border of annuals and perennials.

We can't emphasize this too much: The time to plant a perfect flower border for April, May, and June is not in April, May, and June or even in January, February, or March. Back east and in other cold-winter climates, you have no choice but to plant annuals (and almost everything else) in spring—and take the bloom when you get it. But here the climate allows—in fact *favors*—planting spring annuals (along with perennials, bulbs, shrubs, trees, and vines) in the fall. You should take advantage of this fact.

What happens is that almost any plant put into the ground in October makes root growth, if nothing else, in the autumn and winter. By spring, the plant may or may not look much bigger than it did in the fall—but its roots will be bigger. With this adequate root system, the fall-planted plant can stand the occasional hot days and other vicissitudes of spring. The same plant of the same apparent size set out in, say, February or March would not have the roots or the constitution to sustain itself as well as the one that was planted in the fall.

The fall-planted flowering plant will enter the spring growth period with momentum built up through the winter. The spring-planted plant of the same species will spend much of the same precious growth time establishing itself.

Experienced gardeners in our low deserts know this pattern well, and they garden by it. They do almost all of their planting in September, October, and November. For one thing, it's cool enough then to work in the garden. The winters are mild enough for the plants to root through fall and winter.

Furthermore, spring in the low deserts of the Southwest often turns into summer so fast that your planting opportunity can be gone before you realize it.

BASIC LANDSCAPING AT THE SAME TIME

If you are wise to the West's seasons, you will do your basic landscape planting in the fall, too. Check your needs for trees, shrubs, and vines. Fall is the best time of the year to plant *most* of them. The exceptions: (1) any shrub, tree, or vine that is tender in frost areas, such as citrus, palms, bougainvilleas, and tropical hibiscus; (2) the deciduous trees, shrubs, and vines (such as roses and fruit trees) that nurseries will sell bare root from December to February (and even these can be a bargain now if you get the varieties you want, and if they are not overgrown in their containers).

In October, petunias are planted in a sunny bathroom garden. Young bougainvillea is against wall.

In following spring, this bright display was result of regular feeding and watering.

Annuals

Here are the annuals that nurseries in the low deserts (Phoenix, Tucson, Yuma, Palm Springs) offer to their fall-planting customers in October. You can find descriptions in the *Sunset Western Garden Book*, or the *Sunset* book, *How to Grow and Use Annuals*.

African daisy
Calendula
Fairy primrose (masses can make tremendous displays in spring colors)
Fibrous begonia
Iceland poppy
Lobelia
Pansy (mixed or separate colors)
Petunia
Phlox (annual)
Salvia
Sand verbena
Snapdragon
Stock
Sweet alyssum
Sweet peas (in small pots)
Viola

Perennials and biennials

The following plants are sold from the same counters in the same way as the annuals. Plant them in fall for spring and summer bloom, just like the annuals. But with reasonable care, most of these plants can live over and bloom again for you the next year and many years thereafter. We also include several biennials that bloom only once but can reseed themselves to keep you supplied with seedlings indefinitely.

Anemone
Bells of Ireland
Carnation
Candytuft
Canterbury bells
Columbine
Coral bells
Coreopsis
Delphinium (get seedlings at this time, not large plants)
Dianthus
Dusty miller
English daisy
Forget-me-not
Gaillardia
Gazania ('Copper King' makes a dramatic show)
Geum
Hollyhock
Jerusalem cherry
Marguerite
Nierembergia
Physostegia
Ranunculus
Scabiosa
Scarlet sage
Shasta daisy
Snow-in-summer
Sweet William
Violet

Colorful Arizona flower display planted in October, bloomed in December, lasted into July.

Blue delphiniums, pink dianthus, pink verbena in raised beds, azaleas in adobe brick-edged bed.

Cool looking, all-white border uses white sweet alyssum, violas, petunias, marguerites.

Garden color

There are going to be particular parts of your garden that are your favorites to use for summertime relaxing and entertaining. Even though these spots have comfort in their favor, don't let them get away with being drab and colorless. Your oasis can be as flowerful as a bed of zinnias, marigolds, or petunias if you take proper care of it. And your landscape can be sculptured and accented with color of your own taste so it will be uniquely your own. The *Sunset* book, *Ideas for Garden Color* will help you in your design. And the paragraph below will tell you how to encourage colorful blooms that may already be started in your garden.

How to encourage colorful blooms

As temperatures rise throughout the Southwest desert, many annuals (such as African daisies, calendulas, petunias, snapdragons, stock, and sweet alyssum) will come into full bloom. To encourage vigorous growth and more profuse bloom, feed plants now with a complete liquid or dry fertilizer. Be sure to keep soil around their roots moist with regular irrigation. Spread a 2-inch-deep mulch of ground bark, cottonseed hulls, or similar mulching material around the plants to conserve moisture.

Tall-growing plants such as delphinium, snapdragon, and stock will probably need staking to prevent them from being blown over. Iceland poppies and Shirley poppies on the other hand do not need support.

Give old perennials a new start

When perennials become woody, slow down in their growth, and produce fewer and smaller flowers than usual, it's time to renew them. In most cases this means lifting and dividing the plants. Replant only the newest outside shoots; discard the old, woody

African daisies come in white, shades of yellow, apricot, rose. Yucca recurvifolia *in background.*

Summer marigolds bloom at edge of Sedona, Arizona terrace. Pinon pine, desert juniper in ravine.

center portions. Burn diseased plants.

These are some of the perennials you can divide in the fall: acanthus, asters, columbine, coral bells, coreopsis, daylilies, English daisies, painted daisies, Shasta daisies, poker plant, violets.

The following perennials are easily propagated by tip cuttings taken in early fall: candytuft, dianthus, geraniums and pelargoniums, lavender, marguerites, santolina. To protect the cuttings during winter, place pots or flats in a location where they're exposed to daylight and some direct sunlight, such as at the south side of the house under a wide overhang or on a porch.

To propagate perennials that do not come true from seed, divide plants or take cuttings. Many kinds of perennials are grown from seed, however; it is the fastest and easiest way—and in fact, it is the only means by which certain perennials can be propagated successfully.

Don't forget fragrance

In the fall, when you're choosing the annuals, perennials, and bulbs that will bring gay color to your winter and spring garden, don't overlook the many kinds that have fragrant blooms—such as the candytuft planting that you see in the photograph on the right of this page.

Some plants waft a sweet, pungent, or spicy fragrance over large areas of the garden, while others must be approached closely if you are to enjoy their scent.

Candytuft fills border with color, fragrance, serves as edging for perennials, pyracantha, palm.

Here we list some plants with fragrant blooms that will delight your nose as well as your eye.

Annuals. Candytuft, pinks (*Dianthus*), mignonette, petunias, stock, sweet alyssum, sweet peas, verbena, and wallflower.

Bulbs and bulblike plants. Freesias, hyacinths, iris, and some kinds of narcissus (jonquil, paper white, Chinese sacred lily).

Perennials. Carnations, sweet William, and violets.

The desert blooms

Some desert plants are so showy and bloom in such large masses that they capture the eye immediately, often from a distance—like the yellow-flowered brittlebush common in the foothills and mountains around Tucson. Other plants are so diminutive and ground-hugging that the only way to see them clearly is to lie flat and face them on their own level; some people call these desert miniatures "belly" plants.

Some perennial and shrubby desert plants bloom intermittently over several months, but most of the desert annuals have a life span lasting only a few weeks from sprouting in early spring to seed formation before summer's heat and drought.

How to grow desert wildflowers

Seeds or plants of most of these wildflowers are not available commercially. Wild plants are protected by law in the state of Arizona and may not be collected without written permission from the landowner, as well as a transportation permit from the state. The fact is, of course, that even if it were legally possible to collect plants, it would hardly be worthwhile, since most of them are extremely difficult to transplant successfully.

There is no state law that prohibits collecting seeds; however, anyone wishing to collect seed on private land should, of course, obtain permission from the owner.

If you want to grow wildflowers in your garden, remember nature's way. Spring wildflowers grow from seeds dropped or carried by wind in early summer. Some of the seeds fall into small crevices,

Desert zinnia has daisylike flowers, is common in foothill areas around Tucson.

others are lightly covered by blown sand. The best wildflower years come after a succession of slow rains in October or November followed by periodic rains through the winter.

You should work up the soil in October and give it a deep soaking. When the soil surface dries, rake it enough to knock down large clods; but don't pulverize the soil into a fine dust. Broadcast seed over the prepared area; cover the seed by raking lightly or by scattering peat moss or ground bark on top. Keep soil surface moist until seeds sprout; water less often as the plants grow.

Wildflowers above are only small sampling of spring blooms on Sonoran desert. L-R: Calycoseris (C. wrightii), Desert star (Monoptilon bellioides), Desert mariposa (Calochortus kennedyi).

Best vegetables for desert gardens

Growing vegetables is a popular gardening activity all over, and the desert is no exception. Vegetables are favorites with both the large-scale and the small-scale gardener. There is no need for a king-sized plot; you can grow a surprising number of vegetables in a space only 10 by 10 feet. And some vegetables have enough ornamental value to combine well with your regular garden plantings.

The all-important fundamental of growing good vegetables is to provide them with all the moisture, nutrients, and sunlight they can get; so you have added responsibility for their care in the desert.

The planting season

September is the month to sow seeds of many vegetable favorites of the Southwest desert. For a continuous supply of fresh vegetables, plant every three or four weeks during the planting season.

If you live at an elevation between 1,000 and 2,000 feet, you can sow seeds of the following vegetables throughout September (at lower elevations wait until after September 15): beets, carrots, Chinese cabbage, endive, leek, head lettuce, leaf lettuce, green onions, radishes, spinach, and turnips. Other vegetables that can be planted at this time but require more room are: broccoli, Brussels sprouts, cabbage, chard, mustard, and fall peas.

Corn. To get a good supply of corn before frost, plant seeds of such varieties as 'Golden Cross Bantam,' 'Golden Security,' 'Iochief,' or 'Ioana' around August 15. Planting at this time will also eliminate the problem of corn borers that are troublesome during the spring in desert regions.

Tomatoes. Tomatoes are a favorite everywhere. In such areas as Yuma and Palm Springs, and in the Imperial and Coachella Valleys, plant seedlings any time from January to March 15. In Phoenix, plant from February 20 to March 15; in Tucson, from March 15 to April 15. In the high desert, plant from April 1 to May 10. Set seedlings into open ground as early as possible during the planting season for your area. This gives plants time to develop fully and to produce a good crop of fruit.

In the low desert, tomatoes begin to ripen two to three months after you plant them. Such varieties as cherry and pear tomatoes and Burpee hybrids may continue to grow and set some fruit through the summer, and then give heavy yields in the fall.

In the high desert, expect a light crop of fruit early in July. Then the hot winds keep production low until temperatures cool. Heaviest production begins in late August and continues until frost.

Your success in growing tomatoes will depend largely on your choice of variety. In the low desert, some of the best kinds are Burpee Hybrid, Earliana, Earlypak No. 7, Improved Pearson, Red Cherry, and Yellow Pear; in the high desert, Beefsteak, Burpee Big Early Hybrid, Improved Pearson, Red Cherry, and Yellow Pear.

Vegetables as ornamentals

Don't overlook the ornamental value of certain warm-season vegetables that can be grown in desert gardens. For good looks, as well as good eating, they must have a rich soil, good drainage, full sun, and ample space.

In low-altitude desert areas, you can set out transplants of the vegetables described below early in the spring. In high desert sections, sow seed indoors 8 to 10 weeks before time to set out plants (after frosts); or buy transplants in flats at the nursery.

Eggplant has large, gray-green leaves, white blossoms, and handsome, glossy purple fruit. Four plants will yield a crop of about 12 eggplants.

Peppers (sweet or bell) have rich green leaves; bell-shaped shiny fruit, green when young, red when mature.

Hot (chili) peppers are usually green (sometimes yellowish) when young, turn red at maturity. Six to eight pepper plants are sufficient for the average family.

Perhaps the most ornamental of all is crimson rhubarb chard, which is easily grown from seed. Use it for foliage in the flower border or as a medium height companion for shrubs. Artichoke, too, is a fine, bold ornamental plant; but it does demand constant spraying to control black aphids.

Cherry tomato in hanging pot trails to 4 feet, produces ornamental as well as fruitful crop.

This neat garden has a wide expanse of lawn, bordered by colorful flower beds. Sunken garden in rear. Large area of green has a cooling effect in a desert garden.

LAWNS AND GROUND COVERS

A thriving green lawn or a lush ground cover in the desert strikes the viewer at once with a refreshing splash of color and a sense of cool, restful comfort. Establishing a grass lawn or a ground cover for your desert garden floor is not as difficult as one would suppose.

A cool green lawn

There are many types of lawn grasses in the United States, and they are classified as cool-season grasses and subtropical grasses according to the climatic characteristics of the region in which they will grow.

Along with the other southern parts of the country, the desert regions are subtropical grass and dichondra areas. Dichondra is the low, flat, and green lawn plant used widely as a walk-on ground cover in Arizona and California.

Bermuda grass seems to be the favorite variety for traffic and desert hot weather; however, it does have a winter dormancy when it looks brown and bleak. On the other hand, the bluegrasses that give year-around color are costly to maintain and soon become invaded by crabgrass and Bermuda. A combination of winter grass and Bermuda makes a fairly good year-around lawn. Some people are willing to spend the time and money it takes to keep a cool-season grass in the subtropical grass country, probably because bluegrass is still looked upon by many people as the only real lawn grass.

A green lawn in the winter

Generally, the most common use for the cool-season grasses in the heart of the subtropical grass country is to sow in fall as winter grass over the subtropical grass lawns. It hides the subtropical grasses' dormant brown color.

The traditional winter grass for generations has been annual rye grass. However, this is not necessarily the best choice. It has its drawbacks: It checks later growth of the permanent grasses; it may leave patches that remain throughout the summer; and it is rather sleazy looking.

Bent grass has proved satisfactory for this purpose in many cases. The texture and blade size of the bents and Bermudas are similar enough to make a uniform-appearing turf. Cutting heights are the same. The bent that lives through the summer will be less obvious than the annual rye that might live through. Bents get more insects and diseases than the Bermuda and need more summer watering. In total, if you want to keep a continual bent-Bermuda combination, it will mean more maintenance effort.

There is also some interest in using the bluegrasses and red fescues annually as they are less competitive.

Planting. Although most of this overseeding is done in October, you can also do it in September. During this month the extra heat starts the winter grass off to faster growth than you could get later.

Before you sow winter grass seed, cut the Bermuda lawn as close as possible with a sharp mower. Next loosen and thin out the thick tangle of runners and dead growth with a rake or with a machine designed for this purpose. Then mow again in several directions. Rake up and remove all the grass clippings.

Broadcast the seed evenly over the existing turf at the rate of 1 to 1½ pounds for every 100 square feet of area. Cover the seed with a ½-inch-deep layer of damp peat moss, finely ground bark, or well composted manure. Rake lightly and water thoroughly.

Keep the newly seeded lawn moist at all times. As the grass becomes established, water more deeply and less frequently, to encourage deep rooting.

When grass is about 1½ inches high, cut it with a sharp mower, and keep it cut to a height of 1½ inches. About a month after sowing, feed with a high-nitrogen fertilizer.

Prevent sunburning of a Bermuda lawn

Sunburn is a common complaint about Bermuda lawns and is usually due to improper mowing. If grass is allowed to grow too long, the top growth shades the lower portion of the stem; and when it is suddenly exposed to sunlight, this lower portion burns and turns brown. This can be prevented if leaf growth at the base of the stem is encouraged by frequent mowing so that the grass never grows more than 1½ inches beyond the established mowing height, and the lower leaf blades get acclimated to strong sunlight.

As is true for grasses in all regions, regular watering and feeding is the key to a successful green lawn. A sprinkler system makes particularly good sense in desert regions.

Ground covers

Ground covers have become a popular part of the landscape, both for their own sake and as cover-ups and lawn substitutes. They can be colorful and lush and can require minimum care. We will see later in this chapter that the desert problems of aridity, wind, and soil erosion can be alleviated through the use of ground covers.

Why ground covers?

In many gardens there are places that need some kind of living carpet but where, for one reason or another, grass won't do the trick. You may want to get away from mowing, or want something that takes less watering. You may want one garden surface to look a little lusher and have a softer texture or deeper pile or nap, or a deeper shade of green; or you may want a seasonal sea of color, and many ground covers will give you this. One of the prime motives for growing ground covers is to cover the ground in shade where grass or dichondra won't grow well.

A place to play is this lawn with several carobs used as informal wind and privacy screen.

Cool green in Palm Springs: lawn, low gravel mound, festuca, with Aleppo pine, bamboo, yucca, fan palm.

There are many ground covers and low shrubs that can be used next to a lawn or as a substitute for a lawn. For the most part, these plants require less maintenance than grass or dichondra and still give the same general visual impression as a lawn.

Most flat-growing ground covers will take some foot traffic—enough so that you can walk across them to weed, cut back, or rake off leaves. But they usually cannot stand up under children's play. If you have to walk regularly through a lawn substitute planting, place some stepping stones in it.

Shrubby-type ground covers are fairly permanent, and once planted will continue to serve for many years. In time the plants may mound up too high or grow too far out over walks. When that begins to happen, thin out and cut back the excess growth.

Prostrate Natal plum planting in Palm Springs shows one of many ways to use it.

Since ground cover plants eventually put a solid layer of branches and leaves over the soil, and since it is next to impossible to do much cultivating when this happens, it is important to prepare the soil before planting as if you were putting in a lawn. Cultivate, remove rocks, incorporate soil conditioner and fertilizer, then rake level and plant.

The solution to desert problems

Temperature. It has been established earlier that climate control is to many the primary function of the desert garden. The ground cover is one of the instruments in reducing hot desert temperatures.

As an example, the refreshingly simple planting of Algerian ivy as a ground cover with deciduous trees provides a charming, restful setting for the Las Vegas, Nevada home in the picture in the lower corner of this page. In addition to its eye-appeal, this planting has several practical aspects. The thick ground cover not only looks cool, but actually helps to lower the soil temperature. It crowds out weeds, and its only maintenance requirements are watering and an occasional trimming. In summer (when the photograph was taken) the trees give welcome shade; in winter, sun floods through between the leafless branches.

Erosion. Preventing erosion, especially on sloping ground, is a problem in many desert gardens. A good ground cover to prevent the strong desert winds and water from blowing or washing away the soil is Hall's Japanese honeysuckle. It performs well in both high and low desert, and requires little care once it is established.

Sprenger asparagus (A. sprengeri) *cascades over large native rocks in Palm Desert, California.*

In Las Vegas garden, trees and Algerian ivy ground cover make unbeatable combination in hot summers.

The dwarf coyote brush in the picture below has sturdy, deep roots that are extremely effective for holding steep slopes. It is a versatile evergreen, looking like a solid, leafy carpet, that seems to adapt well to the desert.

It takes fast growth to cover the scars quickly on a steep bank. If you have such a situation, consider the acacia as one of the adaptable plants for use when there's a need for rapid cover to check soil erosion or to provide a quick screen to hide unpleasant views.

Special care in the desert

In the desert, ground cover maintenance has some special problems. The worst problem is Bermuda grass invasion. Best chemical control is to use dalapon mixed with a wetting agent, sprayed on several times in the spring while Bermuda grass is most active. It is important that the spray covers only the leaves of Bermuda. Heavy applications washed into the soil will kill plant roots. Follow label directions.

Another way to control Bermuda's growth in a ground cover planting is to use thick mulches between the ground cover plants while they are growing. Finally, you can try pulling the Bermuda by hand, but complete eradication is almost impossible this way.

The mulching of ground covers accomplishes some other desirable ends. First, it keeps the soil cooler; second, it reduces the possibility of other weeds growing there; and third, the mulch adds a neat decorative touch to the area. Most practical mulch materials are medium and coarse-ground bark, various grades of gravel, or a layer of composted manure.

Watering is very important, since many ground covers grow shallow roots at first. Keep the soil moist at all times. If salinity is a problem, make every third irrigation extra heavy to carry off salts that have accumulated.

A fertilizer program is advantageous in that plants cover more quickly and keep renewing growth. Use ammonium sulfate in frequent, light applications.

Ground cover plots in California City (1) Prostrate germander, (2) Verbena 'Linda', (3) Lavender cotton.

Dwarf coyote brush thrives in planting amid granite rocks near Mojave, California.

Poolside plants reflected in Sun City, Arizona pool include junipers, Japanese black pine, Natal plum, umbrella plant, Myrtus communis *'Boetica'.*

PLANTING AROUND POOLS

In the Southwest desert, many gardeners take advantage of the cooling and relaxing effect of water—especially appreciated during the hot, dry summer months—by installing pools in their gardens. On these four pages, we show you some pools and their plantings that may give you ideas for your own garden.

Ornamental pools

There is a great deal of precedent for the use of pools as ornamental features in the landscape theme of desert gardens. The idea of the use and importance of water was adapted from many cultures but ultimately traced from the eastern countries of India, Persia, and Egypt. In these countries, practically all landscape themes center around a body of water of some size or shape. In a hot, dry country, the sight and sound of water give the comfortable impression of coolness.

Ornamental pools can take either an artificial or a naturalistic setting. The pictures on these pages show both. Water in an artificial setting, such as the pool in the Japanese garden on the opposite page must stay true to its own design and theme. On the other hand, the successful naturalistic setting involves responsibility to the pool's greater surroundings—the desert. The choice of plants and rocks for such a pool is very important. They must have the size and character to look indigenous to the desert. By studying your natural surroundings, you can get a feeling of how nature creates an impression and then copy her.

Swimming pools

The popularity of the swimming pool in desert areas is indisputable. If you have such a prominent item in your landscape, why not incorporate it into your garden scheme as a central or terminal feature? Water in any form focalizes attention to a given spot. Take advantage of this and make that spot the most important and attractive one of your garden.

Pictures of swimming pools on these pages show

what can be done to make your pool more than a recreational area in your garden. Note also the swimming pool on page 18 to see how well a pool can fit into a strictly natural desert setting.

There are two special problems that have to be considered in planting around a swimming pool: litter in the pool and chlorine damage to plants. They are discussed here.

Shade trees for swimming pools

Direct sun can be unbearable around a swimming pool in the high and low desert areas. A lanai or covered patio provides a shady area where you can sit, but carefully chosen and well located shade trees also serve the purpose. *Cordyline australis*, Peruvian pepper (*Schinus polygamus*), African sumac (*Rhus lancea*), and fan palms (*Washingtonia*) in clumps of three or four, are all medium-sized, relatively clean trees that can be planted around a swimming pool. Plant trees at least 20 feet away from the edge of the pool to avoid excess litter and too much direct shade on the water. Locate trees on the downwind side from the prevailing wind, so any litter produced will not blow in the pool.

Avoid planting trees that drop large quantities of flowers, fruit, or leaves, since they will create a maintenance problem, both on the deck and in the pool.

Chlorine damage to plants

Poolside plantings may begin to show chlorine damage in the summer as swimming pool use increases and harmful salts from splashed water accumulate in the soil.

You can minimize this damage by putting the plants in raised beds, or by using a strip of stones to separate pool and planting, as shown on the next page, in a garden designed by landscape architect L. K. Smith. In this planting Korean grass covers the ground at the base of a multitrunked, soft-tipped yucca (*Y. gloriosa*).

If you are planning a new pool, consider having your landscape architect or pool contractor install

Cool refreshing sight and sound of cascading water add to pleasure of swimming in this pool.

OWNER-DESIGNER: MITS MURAKAMI

Placid Japanese garden pool reflects light from lantern. Trailing rosemary softens bridge.

DESIGN: ANDRE CUENOUD

Camelback Mountain makes dramatic backdrop for pool plantings: Natal plum, Queen and Mexican blue palms.

Oleanders steal show when blooming; dwarfed Aleppo pines in corner of pool patio perform all year.

Gravel strip next to pool coping catches most of the water splashed from the pool, protects plants.

a system of drains in or near the decking to carry away chlorinated water.

Planting right beside your pool

If you want to avoid a harsh, barren effect around your swimming pool, you can do it by eliminating the decking along one side of the pool and planting almost to the water's edge. This gives the pool a much more natural appearance and lets it blend with the rest of the landscape. A masonry wall, built flush with the side of the pool, separates the planting area

from the pool and keeps the planting out of range of most of the splashing water.

In most cases it isn't difficult to add this kind of planting bed to your present pool, following the details shown in the drawing below. You should consult a pool contractor or landscape architect, however, before removing the coping and decking. (Most city or county building departments require a 4-foot-wide, solidly paved deck around pools that are built in expansive clay soil.)

If you're planning a new pool, you may want one or more of these planting beds in the design.

Planting behind masonry wall next to pool adds beauty, eliminates an unneeded deck.

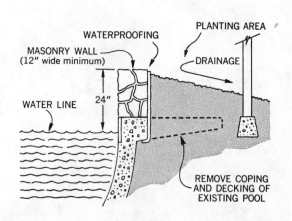

Pool wall in cross section: After removing the coping and deck, add masonry wall.

What to plant around pools

The first list below is of plants to grow around swimming pools. They should be as litter-free as possible and lack bristles or thorns. Broad-leafed evergreens are best for this purpose as deciduous leaf fall and conifer needles make too much mess.

The second list is of plants for small garden pools. Choose plants from this list if the pool is watertight.

SWIMMING POOLS

Trees:

Callistemon citrinus (zones 12, 13)
Chamaerops humilis (zones 10, 11, 12, 13)
Cordyline australis (zones 10, 11)
Magnolia grandiflora (zones 10, 11, 12)

Tall background or screening plants:

Carissa grandiflora (zone 13)
Ilex (holly) (zones vary with kind)
Juniperus (all zones)
Ligustrum japonicum (all zones)
Ligustrum lucidum (all zones)
Nandina domestica (all zones)
Phormium tenax (all zones)
Pittosporum (zones vary with kind)
Viburnum tinus (zones 10, 11, 12)

Low border plant or tall ground cover (to 3 feet):

Agapanthus (zones 12, 13)
Juniperus (all zones)
Moraea iridioides (zones 10, 11, 12, 13)
Pyracantha (all zones)
Rosmarinus officinalis 'Lockwood de Forest' (all zones)

Medium-sized shrubs (4 to 5 feet):

Carissa grandiflora 'Tuttle' (zones 12, 13)
Ilex (holly) (zones vary with kind)
Juniperus (all zones)
Pinus mugo mughus (zones 10, 11)
Pittosporum (zones vary with kind)
Pyracantha (all zones)
Raphiolepis (zone 10)
Rosmarinus officinalis (all zones)
Strelitzia reginae (zones 12, 13)
Xylosma congestum (zones 10, 11, 12, 13)
Yucca gloriosa (all zones)

Vines:

Ficus pumila (all zones)

Japanese iris blooms in May in Tucson garden pool. Waterlilies bloom later.

SMALL GARDEN POOLS

Plants that provide colorful flowers and/or fruits:

Ajuga (all zones)
Canna (all zones)
Cornus (dogwood) (zone 10X)
Hemerocallis (daylily) (all zones)
Iris kaempferi (all zones)
Mahonia (all zones)
Moraea iridioides (zones 10, 11, 12, 13)

Interesting foliage patterns:

Chamaerops humilis (zones 10, 11, 12, 13)
Cyperus alternifolius (zones 12, 13)
Philodendron selloum (zones 12, 13)
Pittosporum phillyraeoides (zone 13)
Salix (willow) (all zones)

Bold forms of large stones contrast dramatically with sword-shaped leaves of Japanese iris.

DESERT GARDEN CALENDAR

January

Annuals

Remove faded flowers to keep plants neat and to encourage more bloom. Sow seeds of ageratum, sweet peas, sweet alyssum.

If you garden at elevations below 2,500 feet, you can plant seedlings of cool-season annuals such as African daisy, calendula, cineraria, pansy, petunia, snapdragon, stock, sweet alyssum, and verbena.

At higher elevations, wait until February or March before planting.

Bulbs and Bulblike Plants

In the low desert, plant gladiolus at two-week intervals for continuous bloom next spring. Plant hybrid amaryllis in pots now for bloom in less than 60 days.

Container and Indoor Plants

Transplant house plants to larger containers if roots are crowded. Carefully loosen compacted roots so that they will grow into the new soil easily. To lessen the shock of moving, water them with a transplanting hormone.

Lawns and Ground Covers

Lawns. Cut and water rye grass lawns. Prepare soil for planting grass and dichondra lawns in March or April. Apply fertilizers and soil-building materials such as peat moss, sulfur, ground bark, composted manure, and phosphorus and potash types; cultivate them thoroughly into the soil. Several disease organisms attack winter lawns causing the turf to die out in patches. See the *Sunset* book *Lawns and Ground Covers* for information on controlling lawn diseases.

Roses

Nurseries still offer bare-root roses for planting this month.

Shrubs

Many kinds of deciduous shrubs are sold bare-root in winter and early spring, and at a lower cost than container plants sold later.

Azaleas. If you received an azalea plant in bloom as a Christmas gift, locate it away from drying drafts while indoors, and keep soil moist. As soon as you can, plant it outdoors in a partially shaded border or (if drainage is poor) in a raised bed.

Camellias. Choose your favorite mid-season blooming camellias at desert nurseries now. This is also the best time for camellia transplanting.

Remove old blooms from established plants, and keep flowers and petals cleaned up from around their bases. To prevent spread of petal blight, burn these flowers.

Gardenias. Can also be planted now; and like camellias, like acid soil.

Trees

Plant bare-root fruit and ornamental trees now.

Citrus. Protect young citrus trees from frost injury by wrapping trunks with palm leaves, corn stalks, or heavy burlap. In windy areas, stake small trees to prevent breakage. You can also protect small trees by mounding up soil high enough to cover the bud union and a section of the trunk. Remove the mound as soon as frosts are over; if you leave it too long, the bark may rot. Don't plant citrus in the garden until after frosts are past.

Vegetables

Lettuce started from seed now will be ready for harvest in about 80 days; from seedlings in about 40 days. You can grow your own seedlings in aluminum loaf pans. Set out plants of artichoke and asparagus.

In the low desert, also sow seeds of beet, carrot, onion, radish, and turnip. Plant tomatoes in warmer low desert areas, but give them frost protection.

Vines

Berries. Prune to remove dead and diseased wood, and thin out old canes to encourage new shoots next spring. Plant bare-root cane berries now. A total of 12 to 18 plants will supply enough berries for an average family.

General Care

Grooming. After their leaves have fallen, prune deciduous trees and shrubs. Cut out congested growth of hardy evergreen trees and shrubs. Treat frost damage, but wait until new growth begins next spring before pruning them; don't even remove frost-damaged branches. Prune roses as soon as buds begin to swell (in the low desert, this is about January 15; in the high desert areas, about March 1).

Mulching. Work into planting beds any leaves you have raked up. As they rot, they provide humus and will eventually return nutrients to the soil. Most desert soils need a pound of sulfur to each sack of mulch.

Watering. Dormant trees, shrubs, and Bermuda grass need winter watering; soak plants about every three weeks. Bermuda grass turns brown in winter, but roots stay alive if watered.

Pest, Disease, and Weed Control

Spraying. Apply dormant spray to fruit trees and cane berries. Select a windless day when there is no immediate threat of rain. Aphids may appear in January on arborvitae and other evergreens as well as on pittosporum; spray with malathion.

Weeds. Winter rains usually bring on a fresh crop of weeds. Hand pull, hoe, or spray with a weed killer (observe all label precautions).

Planting or Transplanting

Plant or move only deciduous or frost-hardy evergreen shrubs, trees, and vines now. If dug carefully, deciduous plants can be moved without soil on the roots. January is the best month to plant bare-root shade trees, shrubs, grapes, and cane berries. Hardy evergreen plants are now about as dormant as they will ever be; move them with as much soil around the roots as you can handle.

February

Annuals

In colder areas, sow seeds of annuals in flats or pots indoors. Keep them in a protected area until ready for transplanting into garden beds. In warm-winter sections, set out transplants of such spring and summer-flowering annuals as African daisies, sweet alyssum, calendula, marigolds, pansies, petunias, snapdragons, and violas.

Bulbs and Bulblike Plants

Anemones and ranunculus, started in flats, are available in some high desert nurseries for planting now. Plant gladiolus at two to three-week intervals for an extended period of bloom. Plant or divide cannas in low desert areas; wait until after frost at higher elevations.

Container and Indoor Plants

Repot indoor plants as soon as roots begin to grow out through the drainage hole.

Lawns and Ground Covers

Lawns. Feed winter lawns about once a month with high-nitrogen fertilizer. Water thoroughly to encourage deep rooting. Wait until March or April before planting dichondra lawns.

Ground covers. Plant as soon as possible to get plants well established before summer heat arrives.

Perennials

You can still plant many perennials such as coreopsis, feverfew, Shasta daisies, and statice (*Limonium*). Water thoroughly after planting, and feed with a complete plant food as soon as growth starts.

Roses

Bare-root and packaged roses will be available in low desert nurseries and garden stores until the end of February, and until March in high desert areas. Buy only plants with pliable roots and plump, healthy canes.

Prune rose plants growing in low elevation gardens about February 15 or when buds begin to swell; in higher elevations wait until about March 15. Remove and burn leaves that have not fallen from rose plants to help prevent spread of disease and insect pests. Form new basins around older plants and apply a mulch.

Shrubs

Azaleas. In sections of the desert where azaleas are grown, soak garden beds, raised planters, and containers regularly to flush out harmful salts. If leaves are yellow, apply iron sulfate or a chelating agent; be sure to follow dosage directions. Plant azaleas in pre-moistened peat moss where they'll get shade and protection from wind.

Camellias. After plants have finished blooming feed with acid-type fertilizers. Mulch older, well established plants with peat moss or ground bark. If rains have been light or your plants are under a wide overhang, give camellias several heavy, deep waterings to flush out salts. If you plan to move a camellia, do it while plants are in bloom; this is the time when plants are most dormant.

Trees

Set out bare-root deciduous trees before new growth starts. When you prune, paint all large cuts with a pruning compound to help prevent disease organisms and insect pests from entering through the cut end. Mulch with composted manure, ground bark, or similar material at the bottom of the watering basin. When leaves begin to sprout, feed trees with a light application of a complete fertilizer.

Citrus. Prune out dead branches, extend watering basins to the drip line of the tree, and irrigate thoroughly and deeply when needed. Continue to protect plants and fruit from frost damage. Wait until after frost before you set out new plants. Begin to fertilize.

Vegetables

In the low desert, sow seeds of beets, carrots, leaf lettuce, onions, parsley, radishes, Swiss chard, and turnips. For rich red color in vegetable or flower beds, plant some rhubarb chard. With protection (under cover), you can start seeds of cantaloupe, cucumber, eggplant, bell pepper, squash, tomato, and watermelon. If you set out tomato plants for an early crop, be sure to place protective coverings over them to prevent frost damage.

In the high desert, you can set out plants of artichoke, asparagus, and rhubarb. Plant seeds of peppers and tomatoes indoors or in a frostproof place.

Vines

Plant hardy vines such as wisteria, silver lace vine, Virginia creeper, cat's claw (*Doxantha unguis-cati*), and Chinese trumpet creeper (*Campsis grandiflora*). Wait until the weather warms before planting tender kinds such as coral vine.

Grapes. Set out bare-root grape plants.

General Care

Fertilizing. Fertilize deciduous fruit and shade trees with a complete fertilizer; water in thoroughly.

Grooming. Wait until new growth starts and weather warms before pruning out frost-damaged stems and branches. Prune spring-flowering lilacs, spiraea, weigela, flowering quince, and flowering peaches immediately after bloom.

In the low desert, complete pruning of roses, grapes, berry vines, and deciduous fruit and shade trees before the end of February.

In the high desert, wait until April to finish pruning these plants.

Watering. Dry winds common in the desert during winter months increase a plant's need for water. Check soil at frequent intervals and water plants thoroughly when needed. Check plants growing in containers or under wide overhangs frequently; water when needed. Newly planted trees, roses, shrubs, and flowers need frequent waterings, even during winter months.

Pest, Disease, and Weed Control

Crabgrass control. To help control this weed, treat the soil in late winter or early spring with a pre-emergence weed killer. If the crabgrass is growing in a dichondra lawn, use AZAC or betasan; if it's growing in a Bermuda grass lawn, use a product that contains any one of the following ingredients: bandane, betasan, dacthal, PMA, AZAC, or methane arsenates. Since crabgrass produces so many seeds that may remain dormant for several years, it may take two or three annual treatments to bring it under control.

Spraying. Apply dormant sprays to deciduous trees and shrubs when needed. When temperatures warm, carefully check plants for build-up of insects and mildew on tender growth, and spray or dust with all-purpose insecticide-fungicide to control.

Weeding. Winter weed growth is often troublesome in desert gardens, especially after rainstorms. Control weeds by spraying with weed killers, hoeing, or pulling them by hand while they are still small. Spray unplanted areas such as drives or walks with weed killers, being especially careful not to get the spray on desirable plants or planting areas.

Weather

Wind protection. Prepare for strong desert winds ahead by staking and tying trunks of young fruit and shade trees, and fastening stems of climbing roses and vines. Re-stake and re-tie older plants.

March

Annuals

Sow seeds or set out plants from nursery flats early in the month. Before you plant, work generous amounts of moist peat moss or ground bark into the soil to a depth of about 8 inches. Sow these kinds in the open ground now: calendulas, Madagascar periwinkle (often sold as *Vinca rosea*), nasturtiums, nicotiana, portulaca, and zinnias. If frost is still a danger, sow seeds in flats and place in a protected area until temperatures rise. Protect young seedlings from the hot sun for a week or two after planting. Thin seedlings before they become crowded.

Feed annuals set out last fall. Mulch flower beds and keep plants well watered. Cut back faded blooms at weekly intervals.

At elevations below 2,500 feet, plant coreopsis, castor bean, cosmos, four-o-clock, gaillardia, globe amaranth, Gloriosa daisy, nasturtium, portulaca, salvia, strawflower, sunflower, tithonia, and zinnia.

Above 2,500 feet, plant sweet alyssum, candytuft, forget-me-not, gaillardia, pansies, painted daisies, petunias, strawflower, and violas.

Bulbs and Bulblike Plants

Pick off faded flowers, but do not remove foliage until it turns to yellow or brown. Cannas are available in dwarf as well as taller-growing kinds. Plant agapanthus, caladium, dahlia, tuberose, and zephyranthes. Plant agapanthus in shaded locations, cannas and dahlias in sun or partial shade.

Gladiolus. Treat plants with an insecticide that contains sevin or diazinon to control thrips. Feed with a complete plant food every three or four weeks before bloom. Do not feed or spray plants while they are in bloom.

Container and Indoor Plants

Container plants. After frost danger, move tender container-grown plants into more open positions.

Indoor plants. To keep plants healthy, feed with light applications of a complete fertilizer at two to four-week intervals. Check plants regularly to determine need for water. Submerge pots every week or two in a pail or tub of water. This saturates the soil and helps flush out harmful salts.

Herbs

Cut back and clean up old growth. Make new plantings as soil becomes warmer.

Feed established plants and water thoroughly. Plant chives, mint, parsley, rosemary, thyme, and sage in loose, well drained soil that contains peat moss or ground bark.

Lawns and Ground Covers

Lawns. Prepare soil for new plantings of Bermuda grass. Bermuda grass lawns that were overseeded with annual rye grass last fall should be cut as close as possible now. Fertilize Bermuda grass lawns with a complete fertilizer, then follow through the growing season with applications of ammonium sulfate.

In warm, low desert areas, plant Bermuda grass seed. Plant plugs or sprigs of hybrid Bermuda grass only after night temperatures remain above 65°. Merion bluegrass sod lawns are successful in California high desert areas.

To control Bermuda mites, spray with diazinon several times or apply 1 pound ammonium sulfate per 100 square feet, water it in, then apply ½ pound dusting sulfur over the same area. Apply complete fertilizer to all lawns. Begin watering regularly. Plant dichondra lawns as weather warms.

Ground covers. Set plants out early so they become established before the weather turns hot. Work up soil, moisten prior to planting. Mulch the open ground between ground cover plants recently set out. In shady areas ajuga and mondo grass grow well. In sunny areas use 'Copper King' gazanias, yellow and orange gazanias, lantana, creeping rosemary, ice plant, or star jasmine.

Perennials

Divide overgrown plantings of ajuga, asters, blue fescue, campanula, chrysanthemums, columbine, coral bells, coreopsis, daylilies, fountain grass, gaillardia, Mexican primrose, and mondo grass.

Chrysanthemums. Divide established clumps and remove excess soil. Replant new shoots from the outside of the clump and discard the old, woody, central portion. Plant the new divisions about a foot apart in well drained soil containing plenty of organic material and superphosphate.

Roses

Spray or dust plants regularly with an all-purpose insecticide-fungicide to prevent diseases and insect pests from damaging the tender new growth. Feed with an iron chelate and a complete plant food as soon as new growth starts.

Bare-root roses may be slow to start growth. Keep the soil moist around their roots. If some of the canes die back, cut them back to a point just above a healthy outside bud, then pack moist peat moss

or sawdust around the canes to help prevent the remaining canes from drying out.

In the low desert, finish pruning your established rose plants by March 1.

At higher elevations, begin pruning as soon as growth buds start to swell.

Shrubs

Set out shrubs while weather is still cool. Provide adequate watering devices, sprinkling systems for shrub borders; don't wait until summer watering needs are critical. From Palm Springs to Yuma, it's safe to plant out such tender materials as bananas, bird of paradise, bougainvillea, ornamental figs (*Ficus*), and hibiscus that need warmth (and water) for fast growth. Cut back frost-damaged elephant ears; they will soon begin to sprout at the base. Keep these plants well watered.

Azaleas and camellias. Apply an acid-type fertilizer as soon as flowers fade. Spade a mulch about 2 inches deep over planting areas to keep roots moist. Water regularly and thoroughly. Move container plants from sunny locations into more shaded places.

Trees

Paint trunks of young trees with tree paint or whitewash (*don't* use an oil-base paint) to prevent sunburn during the summer months. Or wrap them with newspaper mat or other material. Place three or four laths or stakes between trunk and covering for air circulation. Tie trees securely to strong stakes to prevent breakage in heavy winds.

Set out trees for shade from large containers if you missed the bare-root planting season. Fertilize well established, mature trees with soil sulfur and ammonium sulfate. Extend watering basins to the drip line. Water regularly and deeply.

Deciduous fruit trees. If buds of newly planted trees are breaking slowly, wrap stems with moist burlap, or polyethylene film. Examine burlap-covered trees frequently; remove burlap as soon as buds begin to open. Mulch basins; in windy areas, apply a layer of gravel over the mulch to keep it from blowing away.

Citrus. As soon as frosts are over, plant new citrus. Watch new growth for aphids, thrips, or spider mites. At first sign of them, wash off the foliage with a strong spray of water from the hose and follow this with an application of a multipurpose insecticide. Prune frost-damaged plants only after new growth is well started.

Feed established citrus trees. Irrigate deeply in mid-March and in late April. In the hot weather period from mid-May through September, water every 10 days to 2 weeks.

Vegetables

In low elevation desert gardens, you can still sow seeds of lettuce, parsley, radishes, and spinach. Also plant seeds of such warm-season crops as snap beans, corn, cucumbers, muskmelons, squash, tomatoes, and watermelon. Set out plants of tomatoes, peppers, and eggplant and cover to protect from frost; early planting is necessary, since plants must set fruit before hot weather. Cherry tomatoes are less affected by hot weather than other varieties. Wait until hot weather arrives before applying a mulch, since summer vegetables need warm soil to produce vigorous, early growth; mulches tend to keep the ground underneath cool.

Vines

Grapes. When new shoots are 5 to 8 inches long, apply sulfur dust or lime sulfur spray to control mildew. Make 3 or 4 applications at 10 to 14-day intervals for thorough control. Begin regular, deep watering, especially in sandy soils.

General Care

Fertilizing. Feed trees, shrubs, vines, lawns, and flower and vegetable beds with liquid or dry plant foods. Be sure to use at recommended rates to prevent burning plants. Apply iron chelates to such plants as bottlebrush, eucalyptus, pyracantha, and roses now to help prevent chlorosis (a nutritional disorder causing leaves to turn yellow with their veins remaining green).

Garden equipment. Be sure lawn mowers, pruning shears, saws, and hoes are sharp and in good working order as you start the busy spring gardening season. Check tank sprayers to be sure that they operate properly.

Grooming. In low and middle elevation desert areas, all deciduous pruning should have been completed by the end of February; in high elevation gardens, no later than the middle of March. Wait until frost-damaged plants begin to grow before pruning them.

Mulching. To help conserve moisture and to reduce weed growth around plants, add 1 to 2-inch-deep mulches of peat moss, ground bark, or well composted manure. Spread a layer of gravel over the mulch to keep it in place during heavy winds.

Watering. Don't neglect it. Rising temperatures and drying winds increase the need for water during the spring months. Check moisture content of soil around roots, and water thoroughly and deeply when this is needed. At each watering, soak the soil well so that moisture will reach the deepest roots of trees and shrubs. Avoid light sprinklings that encourage surface rooting.

Pest, Disease, and Weed Control

Disease and insect control. Inspect plants regularly for infestations of disease and insect pests. Watch for aphids, thrips, and mildew on tender new growth of roses, trees, shrubs, bedding plants, and spray or dust with an insecticide-fungicide when necessary. Control cutworms and armyworms that damage and often kill young transplants; apply diazinon or sevin at recommended rates. Also bait for snails, sowbugs, and earwigs.

Weeds. Control weeds while they are still young. Soak the soil a day or two to soften the soil before hand-pulling.

Planting or Transplanting

If you live in the high desert, continue to plant bare-root roses, shrubs, shade and fruit trees.

In the low desert, plant asparagus, artichokes, and cane berries as soon as possible. Gardeners in the higher altitudes still have another month to set these plants out.

Be sure to keep all these plants moist with regular, deep watering. Start feeding when growth begins.

Weather

Winter frost damage. Do not prune frost-damaged plants until new growth appears. Many plants that appear to be dead may grow again from the base. Do not fertilize or water heavily plants that have suffered severe frost damage until balance between root and top growth has been re-established, and plants are capable of using normal amounts of water and fertilizer.

Wind protection. Tie young trees to sturdy stakes to prevent strong winds from blowing them over. Also thin out excessive growth of large trees and shrubs to reduce wind resistance. Secure vines and climbing roses to their supports.

April

Annuals

April means late spring in all parts of the desert. Since there's not much time between the last frost and the hot summer sun, spring-blooming flowers must be rushed into the garden in almost-ready-to-bloom shape. After planting, mulch seedlings with ground bark or peat moss and water with a dilute solution of a transplanting hormone. Protect tender young plants from mid-morning and afternoon sun for first 7 to 10 days.

In the low desert, set out amaranthus, balsam, carnations, kochia, marigolds (dwarf types), nasturtium, nicotiana, periwinkle, and portulaca—preferably as small established plants from pots or bands.

In the high desert, plant seeds of fast-growing annuals such as African daisies, sweet alyssum, amaranthus, cosmos, kochia, larkspur, portulaca, snapdragons, and zinnias.

Bulbs and Bulblike Plants

While leaves are still green, fertilize bulb plantings with complete fertilizer. Remove brown leaves of bulbs entering dormancy. Remove faded iris blooms. Plant cannas and dahlias; both grow fast as temperatures increase, and provide a long season of bloom. Tuberoses are generally available for April planting.

In the low desert, buy gladiolus corms now and refrigerate them at 40°. Plant them in August for flowers in October and November.

In the high desert, plant gladiolus at two or three-week intervals for continuous summer bloom.

Cactus

Feed with a light application of a complete fertilizer. Be sure to water the dry plant foods into the soil with a thorough irrigation. Repot container-grown plants if necessary, or plant in garden beds.

Lawns and Ground Covers

Lawns. Plant plugs or sprigs, or stolons of hybrid Bermuda, St. Augustine, and zoysia grasses. Sow seeds or plant plugs of common Bermuda grass and dichondra. Warm nights as well as warm days are needed to germinate Bermuda grass. Although seed planted now will germinate eventually, you won't have a good turf any sooner than you would by waiting until about May 1. Feed established lawns with a high-nitrogen fertilizer. Do not feed overseeded Bermuda grass lawns until the winter grass dies down and the Bermuda grass starts to turn green.

In the high desert, wait until May 15 to sow or plant any of these.

Water and mow regularly. Begin to control Bermuda mites now with applications of soil sulfur and sprays that contain a miticide such as diazinon.

Lippia ground cover. Plant lippia as soon as possible to get growth by summer. Topdress established plantings with weed-free composted manure or a light application of complete fertilizer. Water regularly to establish a thick mat by summer.

Ornamental Grasses

Cut back pampas grass early this month to encourage new growth. Remove unwanted seedlings of fountain grass.

Perennials

Plant carnations, chrysanthemums, gazanias, gerberas, Shasta daisies. Plant coral bells in partial shade.

Chrysanthemums. Make tip cuttings of new growth for bloom in fall. Feed plants now with light applications of a complete fertilizer and iron chelate.

Geraniums. Plant in 8 or 10-inch-wide containers or garden beds for summer color. Protect from hot mid-morning and afternoon sun in the hottest areas. Pinch shoots back to encourage bushiness. Avoid overwatering: allow soil to dry between irrigations.

Roses

Set out container-grown roses. In areas where roses are growing and blooming vigorously, feed with complete fertilizer, water generously, mulch with ground bark, composted manure, cottonseed hulls, or dried clippings. Spray or dust to control aphids and thrips. Many varieties of roses are available in containers at nurseries.

April is the month of roses in lower desert altitudes. Many nurseries put on shows this month as roses planted in containers early this year come into full bloom. By making selections now, you can have established roses in bloom immediately. Northern Arizona gardeners can still plant bare-root roses.

Shrubs

Evergreen shrubs planted this month will establish their roots before high summer temperatures arrive.

Azaleas and camellias. Begin feeding with acid fertilizer. Water thoroughly as temperatures rise. Protect plants from heavy winds. Shade newly planted azaleas and camellias. Mulch to keep roots cool. Cut back rangy plants slightly to encourage more flowering wood.

Gardenias. Apply acid fertilizer to green up plants after a cool winter. Correct chlorosis with iron chelate or ferrous sulfate. Move container-grown gardenias into partial shade.

Trees

Plant evergreen trees as soon as possible to give them full benefit of the long growing season.

Deciduous fruit and shade trees. As new growth begins, trees draw heavily on soil moisture. Increase watering this month and continue into the summer months. Protect the trunk and any exposed branches of young trees from sunburn by painting them with whitewash or covering with mats made of newspapers or similar material.

Citrus

Citrus. April is an ideal month to plant citrus in the mild-winter areas of the Southwest desert. Nurseries have a good supply of citrus trees ready for planting —field-grown, balled-and-burlapped, as well as container-grown plants. Water established trees every other week. Water newly planted trees (if in fast-draining soil) twice a week in normal summer weather. Protect trunks of young citrus trees from sunburn.

Vegetables

Feed vegetables planted earlier in the season with plant food.

In the low desert, keep crops growing steadily with regular watering and fertilizing. Sow seeds of cantaloupe, corn, cucumbers, squash, muskmelon, okra, peanuts, and radishes. Nurseries carry transplants of eggplant, peppers, and tomatoes.

In the high desert, there is still time to plant seeds of warm-weather vegetables. By the middle of this month, with danger of killing frosts past, you can set outplants of corn, cucumber, melon, and pepper; also onion sets and seedlings of broccoli, cabbage, and tomatoes.

Vines

For quick summer shade, plant seeds of fast-growing annual vines (or perennial kinds used as annuals). Among those you can sow now are: Australian pea vine, balloon vine, canary–bird flower, cup-and–saucer vine, cypress vine, hops, moonflower, morning glory, and scarlet runner bean.

Gourds. Plant seeds in full sun after the ground is warm. Give the plants a deep regular watering. Train on wire or trellis against a fence or wall.

General Care

Fertilizing. Feed trees, shrubs, roses, annuals, perennials. Apply fertilizer on all plantings, and feed container plants with complete fertilizer. Be sure soil is moist before applying. Where possible, scratch the dry forms into the soil around plants and always water in immediately after application. Use iron sulfate or iron chelate around plants such as roses, pyracantha, bottlebrush, and citrus to help prevent chlorosis during the late spring and summer months.

Grooming. After new growth starts, remove frost-damaged or dead wood from such tropical or subtropical plants as bougainvillea, Natal plum (*Carissa*), citrus, ornamental fig (*Ficus*), hibiscus, lantana, and yellow oleander (*Thevetia*). Cut back old stems of fern asparagus (*A. plumosus*) to encourage new growth. Cut back marguerites lightly to extend the flowering period. Strip off dead leaves on cordyline, dracaenas, and yuccas; remove dead palm fronds.

You can prune flowering trees and shrubs while they're in bloom and use the branches for indoor arrangements. Cut back scraggly growth on evergreen trees, shrubs, and hedges. Also remove suckers from such trees as citrus, olive, and elm. Paint or spray all cuts that are larger than 1 inch in diameter with a sealing compound.

Mulching. Spread a 1 to 3-inch-deep mulch of ground bark, peat moss, or well composted manure in flower and vegetable beds and in watering basins around trees and shrubs. A layer of gravel on top of the mulch will hold it in place and helps reflect heat.

Watering. Syringe plants and water lawns and garden plants during the early morning hours. Let water run slowly into basins so that it will penetrate deeply into the soil and carry excess salts below the root zone. See that watering basins around fruit and shade trees, shrubs, and roses extend to the drip line. Build the rim of the basin 3 to 6 inches above the surface of the ground.

Pest, Disease, and Weed Control

Begin now to control pests and diseases by spraying or dusting with insecticides or fungicides—or a multipurpose preparation containing both kinds of materials. To help prevent build-up of diseases and insect pests on plants, syringe stems and leaves with a strong jet of water two or three times a week. This is particularly helpful in control of spider mites on such plants as roses, pyracantha, cypress, arborvitae, and junipers during hot weather. Syringe with a strong jet of water in the early morning; spray with a miticide when needed.

Aphids are very active in April. Once a week is minimum spraying for control of aphids on shrubs, roses, and annuals. Diazinon can be used for both aphids and spider mites.

Control thrips on citrus. These nearly microscopic insects usually appear during spring flowering and again in late summer. Injury, evidenced by distorted leaves and scarred fruit, is especially severe on young citrus. Control by spraying with malathion during petal fall.

Weeds. Control weeds before they get too large. In areas where you expect to sow a lawn, water to bring up the weeds, then hoe them off. With some weeds, such as puncture vine, which will soon make its appearance, the less you disturb the ground, the less chance that weed seeds will germinate. A thick mulch of organic matter is the best way to discourage weeds in beds or borders, or around individual trees or shrubs. On paths, asphalt paper covered with a layer of gravel makes an effective and neat-looking weed deterrent.

May

Annuals

To encourage more bloom on such annuals as petunias and sweet alyssum, remove faded flowers and cut back rangy growth. Feed with light applications of a complete fertilizer and water regularly. Set out transplants of amaranthus, celosia, marigolds, Madagascar periwinkle, portulaca, verbena, and zinnias. Do not let plants or seedbeds dry out. Shade plants from the hot sun for a week or two while their roots are becoming established.

In the high desert, you can still plant seeds of summer-blooming annuals such as African daisy, aster, amaranthus, calendula, candytuft, clarkia, gypsophila, marigold, nasturtium, stock, and zinnia.

Bulbs and Bulblike Plants

Feed spring-flowering bulbs with a complete plant food until foliage dries. Some bulbs perform better if they are lifted from the ground and stored during their dormant season. Plant gladiolus, dahlias, and tuberose (*Polianthes*) for bloom in summer and early fall. Set stakes for dahlias as you plant the tubers to prevent injuring them later.

Container Plants

Plants that have been grown in the same containers through two growing seasons probably need to be moved to larger containers as soon as possible. Once a month leach excess salts from the soil by filling the container with water several times and allowing it to drain through the soil. Feed plants lightly at regular intervals.

Plants growing in containers require more frequent waterings than those growing in the ground. Mulch the soil surface with peat moss, coarsely ground bark, or leaf mold, and water frequently —as often as once or twice a day in hot, windy weather.

Lawns and Ground Covers

Subtropical grasses such as hybrid Bermuda, zoysia, and St. Augustine grow vigorously in hot weather. Plant them from stolons, sprigs, plugs, or sod. Sow seed of dichondra. Fill in bare spots by seeding or plugging. Water and feed regularly. Use selective sprays to kill Bermuda grass in dichondra lawns. Mow when grass blades are dry and remove clippings. Cut Bermuda to a height of ½ inch to prevent thatch from building up. Mow zoysia grass between ½ to 1½ inches high, St. Augustine grass 1½ inches high, and dichondra 2 inches high.

If your Bermuda lawn remains yellow after applications of a fertilizer high in nitrogen, the grass may be affected with chlorosis and should be fed with iron chelate or iron sulfate.

Spray Bermuda lawns with a product such as diazinon to control Bermuda mites. Continue to plant summer lawns and to fill in any bare spots in newly planted lawns. If there are low areas in your Bermuda lawn that are less than 3 inches below the desired level, fill in with good soil mix, firm it down, and keep moist. The Bermuda grass will grow evenly through the covering.

Perennials

There's still time to make tip cuttings of chrysanthemums. Pinch back older established plants to encourage branching; give them lots of water. Cut back faded flowers on dusty miller and marguerites. Nurseries carry perennials in gallon containers and smaller pot sizes. Dusty miller, 'Copper King' gazania, rudbeckia, Shasta daisy, salvia, and verbena are top performers in all desert areas.

Roses

Feed every four to six weeks with complete fertilizer containing iron chelate to prevent chlorosis. Water thoroughly; maintain a thick mulch. Cut blooms regularly to encourage more flowers. Tie stems of climbing roses to sturdy supports to prevent the wind from breaking them. Train main stems horizontally against a fence or wall for more profuse bloom. Syringe plants with water, and spray or dust when needed.

Shrubs

Azaleas, camellias, and gardenias. Keep the soil around their roots moist. Shade from the hot sun and protect from strong winds that whip branches. Plant in a loose, fast-draining soil that contains at least 50 per cent organic matter. If your soil drains slowly, plant in containers or raised beds. Feed with an acid-type fertilizer at monthly intervals.

Poinsettias. Cut plants back to about 12 inches high. To increase your supply of plants, take cuttings now. Make them about 6 to 8 inches long, with four to six buds. Allow them to dry in a shady place for several days to seal ends. Then place in sand or other rooting medium so that two or three buds are above the soil. Keep moist and protect from sun until cuttings have developed a good root system. Transplant to pots or sunny garden beds that are sheltered from winter frosts.

Trees

Both evergreen and deciduous trees, especially those planted recently, need watering in large basins. If you have not already done so, apply asphaltic tree paint to large pruning cuts. Check ties to be sure they do not cut into the bark of expanding trunks or branches.

Deciduous fruit trees. Newly planted trees will be making their first real growth as new roots take hold. Check soil moisture about 12 inches below the surface. If the soil crumbles (won't stick together when compressed in your hand), it's time to water. Prop up long, straggly branches as they become heavy with fruit and adjust branches to help shade the fruit from the hot sun. If peach trees are setting too much fruit, thin now to increase both size and quality. Protect trunks of young or newly planted trees from sunburn with whitewash or palm fronds.

Citrus. Continue to protect trunks against sunburn. Water regularly to keep soil moist. In warmer areas, water container-grown citrus in sunny locations daily. Control aphids, mites, and mealy bugs with malathion. Bait or spray for snails and slugs. Maintain a mulch. Don't be alarmed if your citrus tree sheds a large number of its blossoms; it can lose up to 98 per cent of its blooms and still set a good crop of fruit.

In mild-winter desert areas, plant citrus. Most young trees begin to bear worthwhile crops two to four years after planting. Grow in a sunny location and in a fast-draining soil to which you have added organic materials such as ground bark or peat moss.

Vegetables

Thin seedlings of vegetables that you sowed earlier this spring. Spray tomato blooms with a fruit-setting hormone for more fruit.

It is late to plant most vegetables in the lower altitudes. The main jobs here are watering; fertilizing; controlling weeds, insects, and diseases; and harvesting the vegetables as they mature. Mulch all vegetable plots.

At an elevation above 2,000 feet, you can still plant seeds of cantaloupe, celery, cucumber, muskmelon, okra, peanuts, pumpkin, summer squash, and watermelon, and set out small plants of eggplant, pepper, and tomatoes.

Vines

If you planted seeds of annual vines last month, provide support (trellis or wire) for them. Use a mild solution of liquid fertilizer for the first two or three feedings; later, use any kind of fertilizer at

MAY (continued)

full strength as recommended on the label. There is still time to plant seeds for summer shade. The perennial vines can be planted at any time; most of them are grown in gallon or 5-gallon containers.

Grapes. Keep shoots tied to sturdy supports. Give final feeding of a light application of a fertilizer that contains nitrogen. (Excessive nitrogen, applied too heavily or too often, results in vegetative growth that produces little fruit.)

General Care

Fertilizing. Actively growing plants need a good supply of nutrients. Give plants frequent light applications of fertilizer every two or three weeks rather than one or two heavy feedings during the growing season.

At monthly intervals feed lawns with ammonium sulfate or other fertilizer containing a high percentage of nitrogen. If you did not do so at planting time, give flowers and vegetables an application of bonemeal or superphosphate by scratching recommended rates into the soil around plants. Be careful not to disturb the roots.

Grooming. In colder areas, cut back frosted plants that are now leafing out, such as bottlebrush, bougainvillea, and lantana. Trim off dead palm fronds.

Mulching. Spread a 1 to 4-inch-deep mulch of ground bark, composted manure, peat moss, or other mulching material around trees, shrubs, plants in containers, vegetable and flower beds to help conserve moisture.

Watering. Watering is the number one garden chore in desert gardens. Practically all kinds of plants except drought-tolerant natives need deep and regular watering. To leach out harmful salts effectively, apply five or six times the amount of water you normally give a plant. Light waterings encourage roots to grow near the soil surface where hot temperature and dry winds easily kill them.

Newly planted lawns, annuals, many container plants, and vegetables may need to be watered one or two times a day to keep the soil moist and to prevent plants from wilting. Established lawns, shrubs, vines, and trees require deep irrigations from twice a week to once every two weeks, depending on the depth of the roots, soil type, and weather conditions.

Pest, Disease, and Weed Control

Pests. Spray early in the morning before the wind comes up and the sun gets hot. Avoid spraying or dusting with sulfur when the temperature rises above 85°.

Hosing off plants with a strong force of water often helps to keep down some pests—aphids for example. Bait for cutworms slugs, snails, and sowbugs.

Chlorosis. Yellowing that usually shows up first between the leaf veins characterizes chlorosis caused by an iron deficiency. Treat the soil around the roots with either iron sulfate or iron chelate.

Weeds. When weeds such as puncture vine make their appearance, pull them out or spray with weed killer rather than hoeing. They come back easily from portions of root left in the ground. Clean up remnants of tumbleweed and remove seedlings as they develop. Elm seedlings sprout vigorously at this time of the year; pull them up while they're still small.

Weather

Sun protection. Shade newly transplanted annuals. Move all except the most sun-tolerant container plants into shade. Protect trunks of small trees by applying cold-water paint or paper trunk bands.

June

Annuals

Mulch existing plantings to keep ground moist. Water deeply, feed every three to four weeks. To encourage fresh new growth and more bloom, cut back leggy stems on such kinds as petunias and verbena. Remove and destroy diseased or spent winter and spring-flowering annuals. Plant cockscomb, cosmos, globe amaranth, Gloriosa daisy, marigolds, tithonia, or zinnias.

In middle and high-elevation desert areas set out balsam, celosia, cosmos, globe amaranth, Gloriosa daisy, kochia, African marigold, Madagascar periwinkle, portulaca, sanvitalia (creeping zinnia), and zinnia.

Bulbs and Bulblike Plants

Clean up remaining dead foliage of spring bulbs. For summer color plant blue and white agapanthus, cannas, dahlias, and tuberose (*Polianthes*), generally available at this time.

Iris. Remove dead leaves. Delay transplanting iris until fall, to prevent rot.

Lawns and Ground Covers

Lawns. Watch lawn color; if it turns from rich green to a smoky bluish color, it's nearing the wilting point. Water it

at once and deeply. If it takes up water very slowly, sprinkle it for a short period, shut off the water, and then sprinkle again.

Control lawn moth and crabgrass. Use selective sprays to control Bermuda grass in dichondra.

Plant dichondra seed. Plant hybrid Bermudas, zoysia, St. Augustine grass from stolons, sprigs, plugs, or sod.

Ground covers. Cut back ajuga to remove faded flower spikes, even-up growth, encourage spreading. Plant heat-resistant ground covers such as bougainvillea, dwarf Natal plum, junipers, low-growing lantanas, sedums, star jasmine, and Peruvian verbena. Mulch new plantings to conserve moisture and check weed growth.

Mint thrives in a shady location with lots of water. It's often slow to start, but once it gets going it can become a pest unless you thin it out and clip it back occasionally.

Perennials

For summer color, plant container-grown dusty miller (*Centaurea*), dianthus, gerbera, and rudbeckia. In the hottest areas, plant geraniums and pelargoniums in a location protected from the hot mid-day and afternoon sun.

Chrysanthemums. Pinch out tip growth to force side branches and make plants bushier. As plants grow taller, stake and tie the stems to prevent damage by strong winds. Plants in containers need watering more frequently than those planted in the ground.

Dahlias. Keep soil around their roots moist but not soggy wet; excess moisture may rot the tubers. Do not feed with heavy amounts of a fertilizer high in nitrogen; you may encourage vigorous foliage but few blooms. Tie stems to sturdy supports to prevent wind damage.

Roses

Water regularly and deeply, preferably in basins. Mulch to reduce loss of soil moisture. Every four to six weeks, apply complete fertilizer containing iron chelate (to prevent chlorosis). Control spider mites, especially serious in hot weather, with a miticide or systemic insecticide that also controls thrips and other sucking insects. Use a multipurpose insecticide to control leaf-eating pests.

You can still set out roses from containers. Place a heavy mulch around newly planted roses and keep them damp at all times until roots become established. Maintain a mulch around older plants.

Shrubs

Feed shrubs to gain rapid summer growth, and mulch to retain moisture. Widen irrigation basins to the drip line.

Azaleas and camellias. Tip-pinch growth to encourage dense branching. Apply acid plant food according to label directions. Leach out salts at least once a month with a long slow soaking. Water regularly and maintain a mulch to keep roots moist at all times.

Hibiscus. Thin or cut back at least one-third of the growth on older plants of evergreen Chinese hibiscus. Also prune younger plants to encourage branching and more flowering wood. Water regularly. Apply complete fertilizer monthly. Since hibiscus need a warm soil, summer is a good time to set them out (in partial shade). Avoid thick layers of mulch that tend to keep the soil cool. This is also a good time to plant the hardy perennial hibiscus (*H. moscheutos*).

Lantana. If you haven't already done so, severely prune woody or frost-damaged plants. Avoid overwatering or excessive fertilizing.

Privet. Keep the blooms cut off to improve the appearance of foliage and the entire plant.

Trees

Hot summer days are the best time to evaluate shade trees. Make notes to help you decide which will suit your particular needs.

Feed to gain rapid summer growth, and mulch to retain moisture. Widen irrigation basins to the drip line.

Deciduous fruit and shade trees. Both need ample water. Provide large basins adequate for deep, thorough watering or use soil soakers. If you haven't already done so, thin fruits to space them well apart on the branch, permit air circulation, reduce danger of rot, and produce larger and better shaped fruits. Support heavily laden branches with poles to prevent breakage.

Citrus. Citrus trees should now be in full flush of growth; pinch tips to keep plants bushy. Use malathion to control aphids, mites, and mealybugs. Increase watering as temperatures rise and growth develops.

Protect trunks of newly planted trees by painting with tree paint or white-wash, or covering with palm fronds. Move container-grown plants into locations protected from the hot morning and afternoon sun. At least once a month, in addition to regular waterings, fill the container with water several times to flush out accumulated salts.

Palms. Plant or transplant this month.

Vegetables

In middle and high-elevation gardens, plant seeds of beets, cantaloupes, carrots, corn, cucumbers, endive, lettuce, parsnip, radish, rutabaga, squash, and watermelon. Tomatoes are still available as small plants.

General Care

Fertilizing. Continue to feed lawns, garden and house plants. Since large doses of fertilizer may burn plants during the hot summer months, it is usually better to feed plants with light but frequent applications.

Grooming. Pinch chrysanthemums to make them bushy. Cut back branches of pyracantha that extend beyond the main body of the plant, particularly on espaliers and hedges. Saw off old palm fronds.

Mulching. Check depth of mulches around trees, shrubs, vines, roses, and in flower and vegetable beds. Add more to maintain the desired depth.

Watering. Don't let plants wilt. Check soil moisture frequently and apply enough water to penetrate deeply into the soil and encourage roots to grow down deep. In working out summer watering schedules for trees, shrubs, and smaller plants, keep these principles in mind: Wet every particle of soil that contains the roots of the particular plants. For a large tree it may mean watering a block of soil 6 to 8 feet deep. Lawns need water to a depth of approximately 1 foot. A small plant may be in a block of soil 1 to 2 feet in diameter and 1 foot deep. The interval between waterings should allow soil to become somewhat dry before more water is applied. Too much water produces chlorosis.

Pest, Disease, and Weed Control

Pests. Spray or dust early in the day before it gets hot and windy. Hose off plants frequently (early in the morning) to help keep them free of certain pests and to wash off dust. If you notice browning and drying tips on junipers, look for twig borers (by scraping the bark at the base of the dead portion you may find tunnels); spray with sevin or diazinon. Control juniper blight, a disease that causes dieback on twigs and branches, with copper sprays. Grubs are now appearing in clover and dichondra lawns. Treat with sevin or diazinon. Also control aphids, thrips, grape-leaf skeletonizer, red spider mites, and cottony cushion scale.

Disease. Warm weather and heavy summer rains encourage root rot, powdery mildew, and other fungi. If trouble is detected early, you can save the infected plant.

At first signs of chlorosis, treat with iron chelate or iron sulfate.

Weeds. Mulches reduce weed growth. Spot treat Bermuda, Dallis, Johnson grasses, velvetgrass, and Alta fescue with dalapon—but do not use it in root areas of established plants. Control crabgrass in grass lawns with weedicide containing phenyl mercuric acetate (also controls certain fungus diseases). Control nutgrass with spot application of 2,4-D.

Annuals

For late summer and fall color, plant cosmos, Gloriosa daisy, dwarf marigold, portulaca, Madagascar periwinkle, and zinnia. Pre-moisten the soil before planting; protect plants from hot sun until they are established. Keep soil moist, not wet. Apply complete fertilizer monthly. Mulch flower beds to keep roots cool, reduce weed growth, and stretch intervals between waterings. Remove spent annuals. To prolong bloom of those that are still flowering, cut off faded flowers. If you have the time and energy, now is a good time to dig, add soil amendments, and soak the ground in preparation for fall planting.

Bulbs and Bulblike Plants

Iris. Clean up iris beds; remove dead leaves; burn diseased leaves and rhizomes affected with rot. Wait until cooler weather in the fall to dig, divide, and replant iris.

Container Plants

To keep soil from drying out in containers and being washed out during watering, apply a 2-inch mulch of pea gravel, coarse bark, or crushed rock over the surface. To reduce salt content in the soil, flush out containers at least once a month with repeated applications of water.

If plants that are growing in a container wilt quickly even when watered every day or so, check to see if they are rootbound. If so, transplant to a larger container and move to a shady location until plants are established.

Protect succulents from direct sun during the hot summer months.

Lawns and Ground Covers

Keep Bermuda grass lawns cut short. Apply summertime crabgrass controls or hand-pull small plants as often as you can. Soak deeply when watering. During this active growing season there is still time to plant dichondra seed, and such grasses as hybrid Bermuda, St. Augustine, and zoysia.

Do not mow dichondra lawns too closely.

Roses

Remove the faded roses regularly to keep new ones coming on. When cutting roses, leave as much foliage as possible on to shade the stem and the base of the plant. Mulch to keep roots cool. Overhead spraying with water in the early morning will help keep the plants free of mites and aphids and reduce mildew attacks.

Trees

Deciduous fruit trees. Their need for water is greatest in summer. Water deeply in basins extending to the drip line of the tree. To prevent sunburn and bark splitting that may encourage such diseases as gummosis, paint trunks and exposed branches with whitewash.

Citrus. Citrus need extra attention during their most active growing and fruit-producing season in the hot summer months. Water deeply and regularly—at least once a week for plants set out this spring, oftener if soil is sandy and drains rapidly; water older, established citrus every 12 to 14 days. Avoid cultivating around basins. Protect young trees from sunburn by wrapping the trunk with burlap or paper or by applying cold-water paint.

Palms. This is a good month to move palms or to plant them from nursery containers.

Vegetables

Water regularly and apply or replenish mulches where necessary.

In the high desert, shade tomato plants whose foliage is sparse—hot sun will burn the fruit.

General Care

Fertilizing. Feed lawns and actively growing plants with light applications of a complete fertilizer; lawns need a high-nitrogen plant food.

Grooming. Trim lower limbs from such trees as mulberry and fig if these pendant branches interfere with traffic of adjacent plants. Thin brittle-branched trees such as Brazilian pepper and elms to prevent wind damage. Cut off dead fronds of palms. Cut back scraggly growth of such plants as lantana and nandina and pinch chrysanthemums to keep them neat and bushy. Cut back faded flower clusters of verbena and Madagascar periwinkle to encourage repeat bloom. Remove unwanted growth of pyracantha.

Keep espaliered plants neat and trim by tieing back or clipping unwanted shoots as they appear.

Mulching. Next to watering, mulching is most important in maintaining a lush summer garden. Mulches help prevent loss of soil moisture, keep plant roots cool, and restrict weeds.

Watering. Don't neglect it. You can lose a recently planted tree or shrub by skipping a single irrigation. Flower beds, lawns, and recently planted shrubs and trees need deep watering every four or five days. Water containers every day—twice a day during extremely hot spells. The ideal time for garden watering is early morning before the sun has had a chance to turn on its full force. Hot sun may burn wet leaves. If you must water during the day, flood-irrigate so water doesn't get on the leaves. (Most plants if watered at night are more susceptible to fungus attack.)

Pest, Disease, and Weed Control

Pests. Syringe plants in the early morning to wash off dust and many disease spores and insect pests from plants. Spray or dust when needed.

Chlorosis. Watch for this common yellowing of plants, the result of iron deficiency. Treat with an iron chelate immediately.

Texas root rot. July and August are months when Texas root rot is likely to appear on trees, shrubs, and some other kind of plants. Wilted leaves are the usual symptoms. Treat affected plants.

Weeds. Control weeds by hand pulling or applying chemical controls. Spray with weed oil around edges of Bermuda lawns to keep the invasive roots from spreading into flower and shrub borders or onto paths.

Trees like Siberian elm send up seedlings and roots sprout readily around the base of the tree. You'll probably be kept busy pulling or digging these out. If in the lawn, you can cut young sprouts off with the lawn mower.

August

Annuals

To keep summer-flowering annuals blooming over a long period, water them regularly, remove faded flowers and dead stems and leaves, and apply a mulch around the plants to keep their roots cool and to retain soil moisture. Where available as well started plants in small pots or flats, you can still set out Madagascar periwinkle and dwarf marigolds for late color. Set out seedling transplants of zinnias in mid-August for bloom from mid-October until frost. Protect young plants from hot sun and drying winds until roots are established.

Bulbs and Bulblike Plants

Iris. To help prevent crown rot, a disease that often attacks iris, water in the late afternoon and keep soil moist but not soggy wet. Cut off dead foliage. Dig out and destroy infected plants.

Cactus

Don't let them dry out during the summer months. If you do, they may become dormant. But if watered too heavily they may rot.

Container Plants

For quick color use bougainvilleas, lantana, and hibiscus, all available as blooming plants in nurseries. Once a month, leach out salts with repeated waterings. Follow up with a feeding of complete fertilizer.

Container plants tend to dry out more quickly than they did earlier in the season due to high summer temperatures as well as because plant roots and top growth have increased in size and require more water.

Lawns and Ground Covers

Water lawns deeply. Mow Bermuda grass lawns as low as possible and remove cut grass to keep thatch from building up. You can still plant hybrid Bermuda, St. Augustine, and zoysia grasses; dichondra seed also grows quickly with warmth and plenty of water. Control crabgrass with a product recommended for this purpose.

Perennials

Sow seeds of spring and summer-flowering perennials such as columbine, coral bells, delphinium, gaillardia, Iceland poppy, and penstemon. Fill flats or clay pots with a porous, well drained soil mixture. Cover the container with clear plastic or a small pane of glass, and keep it in the shade. When the seeds germinate, bring seedlings into a well lighted but not full-sun area, and remove cover. When the second set of true leaves appear, transplant seedlings to another flat filled with a richer soil mix. Space seedlings 2 to 3 inches apart. Keep soil moist until plants ure ready to set out.

Roses

Deep watering and another feeding this month will help prepare plants for fall flowering. Replenish mulches. Keep up a regular watering schedule throughout hot weather. Remove faded flowers. Thin and tie up canes of climbing roses. Apply complete fertilizer to encourage the second flowering season during fall. If plants show signs of chlorosis, apply iron sulfate or chelates. If necessary, spray or dust for spider mites with a preparation that contains diazinon, kelthane, malathion, ovex, or tedion.

Shrubs

Azaleas, camellias, and gardenias. Protect from hot sun. Feed with an acid-type fertilizer and iron chelate to encourage vigorous growth and the formation of buds that will produce next season's bloom. Maintain a 2-inch-deep mulch around roots.

Trees

Citrus. Irrigate every 10 to 14 days by slowly filling the watering basins that extend to the drip lines of the trees. Plants growing in containers need more frequent watering. Keep weeds and grass out of the watering basins (particularly around young trees). If a tree is growing in a lawn, apply a fertilizer that is high in nitrogen and phosphorus to keep both tree and lawn healthy.

Dates. Place protective coverings over the clusters of developing fruit to prevent insects and moisture from damaging them. You can get date bags at nurseries and garden supply stores.

Palms. Keep palms well watered and apply a complete fertilizer now while growth is rapid. August is a good month to set out new palms or to transplant established ones. When transplanting, tie the outer fronds together with twine to protect the inner growth bud from the drying effects of the hot sun and wind.

Vegetables

Seeds of snap beans, peas, and radishes can go in now. Prepare soil for fall planting.

General Care

Fertilizing. Feed all plants in active growth regularly with a complete dry or liquid fertilizer. Follow label directions closely. Light feedings applied regularly are safer and more effective than heavy doses at irregular intervals. Feed Bermuda lawns every six weeks with ammonium sulfate at the rate of ½ pound per 100 square feet. Water in thoroughly immediately after applying.

Grooming. To prevent wind damage from summer storms, thin out dense growth of such trees and shrubs as California pepper tree, evergreen elm, mulberry, silk oak, and African sumac (*Rhus lancea*). Wait until winter before you do any heavy pruning. Prune unwanted growth of mulberry, myrtle, pyracantha, and xylosma. Remove suckers on lilacs, roses, and fruit trees. Pinch chrysanthemums and dahlias to encourage side shoots; stake tall stems.

Mulching. If wind, rain, or irrigation water has washed or blown mulches away from around plants or out of planting beds, add more to help conserve moisture and reduce weed growth.

Watering. Water flower beds and lawns at least twice a week. Deep-soak citrus, fruit and shade trees at 1 to 2-week intervals, depending on soil texture, weather, and size and condition of the plant. Plants in containers need more frequent watering.

Pest, Disease, and Weed Control

Syringe plants regularly with a strong jet of water to keep them clean of dust and to wash off some insects and disease spores. If the infestation is heavy, spray or dust with an insecticide, miticide, or fungicide. Spray with malathion to control red spider mites. Pyracanthas, arborvitae, and chrysanthemums are quite susceptible to this pest.

If lawn moth larvae (sod webworms) cause brown patches in your lawn, treat with sevin, dibrom, or diazinon. Spray lawns with a preparation such as diazinon to control Bermuda mites.

Texas root rot. This fungus disease is most active in July and August. If a well watered tree or shrub wilts suddenly, suspect Texas root rot; prompt treatment can often save the plant. Immediately dig a basin around the tree or shrub as far out as the end of the branches, and spread a 2-inch layer of manure in the basin. Then scatter ammonium sulfate and sulfur over the manure, at a rate of 1 pound of each every 10 square feet, and irrigate deeply. Cut back the plant severely.

Weeds. Remove weeds before they form seeds. If you pull weeds while the soil is wet, the job will be easier, and you also have a better chance of removing the entire root system.

Weather

Sunburn. Prevent sunburn on trunks of young trees by wrapping them with palm fronds or by painting them with whitewash or a white tree paint.

September

Annuals

Prepare soil for the annuals that you intend to plant this fall. Plant seeds now; set out nursery transplants as soon as available. Protect seedlings from hot sun and wind for a week or two after planting; keep roots moist. Set plastic strawberry baskets over young plants to protect them from birds. Cut back scraggly or matted growth on petunias and verbena.

Everlasting blooms. Cut flowers of these everlastings when they reach full bloom: plume cockscomb (*Celosia*), globe amaranth (*Gomphrena*), strawflower (*Helichrysum*), and statice (*Limonium*). Take as much stem as possible, and strip off foliage for easier handling. Wrap bunches in a newspaper cone and hang upside down in a warm, dry, well ventilated place. They will be ready for use in arrangements in about three weeks.

Sweet peas. Plant seeds of sweet peas of early-flowering kinds now for winter bloom. These include Multiflora (vining type) and the Bijou and Kneehigh strains (bush type). Flower colors include white, soft pink, bright rose, scarlet red, pale blue, and shades of salmon.

Bulbs and Bulblike Plants

Buy the bulbs you wish to plant as soon as they are available (for best choice), then wait until daytime temperatures cool before planting them.

Store hyacinth and tulip bulbs in the vegetable drawer of your refrigerator for four to six weeks before planting.

Iris. Divide crowded iris clumps and set out new rhizomes; trim leaves back to about 6 inches on newly-planted rhizomes. Plant in raised beds, or where soil is fast draining and high in organic matter. Plant single rhizomes (not clumps) about a foot apart, with the leafy end of the rhizome pointing in the direction you want growth to take. When replanting, cover the young rhizomes with ½ to 1 inch of good soil mix, and keep them moist, but not soggy wet.

Lawns and Ground Covers

Keep lawns neat and in active growth with regular mowings, thorough irrigation, and monthly feedings with fertilizers high in nitrogen. Water the lawn well the day before you apply fertilizer and water immediately after application. Eriophyid mites that cause tufting and yellowing of Bermuda lawns are still active at this time; control with diazinon.

This is the last month this year to plant dichondra lawns. Water and feed existing lawns. Hold off feeding Bermuda grass if you intend to overseed it with a winter grass. During the last two weeks of September and in October, begin planting new lawns with cool-season grasses and overseed summer lawns for a green turf during the winter months.

Perennials

Chrysanthemums. Stake tall-growing varieties and exhibition types with large, heavy flowers. If you want the largest possible bloom, disbud the large-flowered kinds, leaving only one bud per stem. Feed plants once a week with a liquid plant food that is diluted to half strength. Stop feeding after flower buds begin to show color. Don't let plants dry out. Mulch to help keep soil moist. Apply water in furrows or basins. Overhead watering makes plants topheavy, increases risk of breakage, and helps spread disease.

If plants have turned yellow during the hot summer, make a light application of complete fertilizer and iron chelate. Plants will green up during the next few weeks.

Geraniums and pelargoniums. Increase your supply of plants by making 3-inch-long cuttings from new growth six to eight weeks after cutting the plant back, or from the tip growth of non-flowering wood. Remove lower leaves and dust end of each cutting with rooting hormone. Place in sand, vermiculite, or similar material, and keep shaded until they are well rooted—in about six to eight weeks. Then plant in 3-inch pots. Protect from winter frosts.

Roses

Don't let plants wilt. Feed with a complete fertilizer or one specially formulated for roses. Prune out dead branches and twiggy growth. In many areas, roses will begin their fall bloom this month. Maintain a 2-inch-deep mulch around the plants. Remove sucker growth that comes from roots and stems below the bud union. Pull out suckers.

Shrubs

Azaleas, camellias, and gardenias. Keep their roots moist at all times. If plants begin to show signs of iron chlorosis (yellow leaves with green veins), apply iron sulphate or iron chelate. Do not fertilize again until after bloom. Disbud camellias by removing two or three buds from each stem to get the largest flowers.

Hibiscus. Hibiscus are in peak bloom now; it's a good time to select and plant them. Plant in a fast draining soil rich in organic matter. Shade from hot sun after planting, and keep soil moist. Protect from frost.

Trees

Deciduous fruit trees. Provide plenty of moisture around the roots of trees. Extend watering basins to, or slightly beyond, the drip line of new growth, and water deeply at regular intervals. Thoroughly irrigate well established trees every 12 to 15 days, and young trees every 7 to 10 days. Cut off sucker growth below the bud union. Prune out broken branches and deadwood. Pick up and destroy all fruit that has fallen around the base of the tree to prevent sour fruit beetles from multiplying in the decaying fruit.

Citrus. Continue deep watering. Wash dust off foliage with a strong jet of water.

When leaves are dry, spray with malathion to control scale and thrips.

Dates. When fruits start to lose their green color, spray them with a preparation of ferbam and sulfur to prevent fungus damage. In late September, spray fruit clusters with malathion to kill the dried fruit beetle that often damages the fruit. Also remove fallen fruit from around base of the tree. Wash harvested fruit thoroughly.

Vegetables

Vegetable planting season begins September 1 in high desert areas and September 15 in lower elevations. Plant seed of beets, carrots, chard, endive, kohlrabi, lettuce, parsley, parsnips, peas, radishes, rutabagas, spinach, and turnips. Later this month set out plants of broccoli, cabbage, and cauliflower. Plant seeds of beets, carrots, lettuce, radishes, and spinach at two or three-week intervals so that you will have a continuous supply during winter and spring.

Pest, Disease, and Weed Control

Control spider mites by washing dust off plants and spraying thoroughly with diazinon. Spray or dust with an all-purpose insecticide-fungicide to control aphids and mildew.

In the high desert, cutworms or armyworms may damage growth of annuals, perennials, and shrubs. Spray with an insecticide that contains diazinon, dibrom, or sevin to control them. Spray or dust with a fungicide as soon as mildew appears.

Chlorosis. Use iron chelate at regular intervals to prevent chlorosis in such plants as roses, bottlebrush, and xylosma.

Weeds. Puncture vine and other weeds should be controlled before they go to seed. Treat with weed killers and be sure to cover the plant completely with spray. When using any weed killer, avoid spraying on a windy day, or if desirable plants are close by. Even grass killers may damage or kill many broad-leafed plants.

General Care

Fertilizing. Feed plants with a fertilizer that contains nitrogen and phosphorus. Water thoroughly after feeding. You might try a fertilizer that contains a systemic insecticide which is absorbed by the roots and travels through the plant and kills many insects that feed on it. But never use this material on vegetables or other edible crops. Since many desert soils are low in phosphate, work in recommended rates of a fertilizer such as superphosphate when you prepare soil for fall planting.

Labeling. Check labels on azaleas, camellias, roses, and trees to be certain they are legible and that label wires and ties are not too tight.

Mulching. See that trees and shrubs, flower beds, and plants in containers are mulched to a depth of at least 2 inches.

Watering. Late summer rains may help supplement your watering program. However, to keep plants healthy and in active growth, irrigate regularly and deeply during dry weather. Water annuals, perennials, container plants, and newly planted shrubs and trees every three days. Lawns and established shrubs need water at least once a week. Water mature trees every 12 to 15 days. Sprinkle newly seeded lawns with a fine spray as often as necessary to keep the seedbed moist.

October

Annuals

Remove summer annuals as soon as they have finished blooming to make room for the winter and spring-flowering kinds you will plant this month.

Feed plants that were set out last month with a complete fertilizer; keep them moist with frequent waterings. Maintain a mulch to prevent the soil from drying out.

Winter and spring-flowering annuals available in nurseries include: African daisies, ageratum, asters, calendulas, candytuft, Iceland poppies, lobelia, pansies, petunias, phlox, snapdragons, stock, verbena, and violas. After planting in good soil mix, spread an inch-deep mulch of ground bark, well composted manure, or peat moss in the planting bed. Shade seedlings from wind and the hot sun for a week or two until they're established. Keep them moist with regular waterings. You can also sow these seeds directly in the ground where they are to grow: anchusa, African daisies, California poppies, coreopsis, clarkia, spider flower (Cleome), summer cypress (Kochia), larkspur, lupine, love-in-a-mist (Nigella), Shirley poppies, sweet alyssum, and wallflower.

In the low desert, continue soil preparation and planting seedlings of such annuals as calendulas, pansies, petunias, snapdragons, stock, and sweet alyssum. Shade newly planted seedlings from the hot sun until they're established.

In the high desert, complete planting annuals by October 15, so that plants will be well established before frosts which will usually begin by November 15.

Sweet peas. Plant seed of the spring-flowering kinds or get seedlings in small pots from nurseries. Seeds germinate quickly when planted in warm soils this month. Plant them about an inch deep in a 12 to 18-inch-deep trench filled with good garden loam and plenty of organic matter. Provide support and protect from birds.

Bulbs and Bulblike Plants

For spring bloom, set out anemones, callas, crocus, daffodil, Easter lily, freesia, gladiolus, hyacinths, Dutch iris, lycoris, ranunculus, sparaxis, and watsonias. (Wait until November before planting tulips.) Store hyacinths and tulips in the vegetable drawer of your refrigerator for at least four weeks before planting. Soak anemone and ranunculus tubers in water for 3 to 4 hours before planting.

Container Plants

Move frost-tender plants to protected areas. Continue to keep soil moist and maintain mulch around plants.

Lawns and Ground Covers

Keep them moist with regular waterings. Apply sevin, dibrom, or diazinon to control lawn moths.

When night temperatures fall below 50°, common Bermuda grass lawns will begin to turn brown and go into their dormant period. (Hybrid Bermuda grasses such as 'Tifgreen' usually stay green longer in fall than the common Bermuda grass.) For a green turf during the winter months, sow such cool-season grasses as annual rye or 'Pennlawn' fescue over the Bermuda. Or dye the dormant turf with a green colorant; this is especially useful on hybrid Bermuda grass lawns whose dormant period is often too short to warrant overseeding.

Perennials

In mild-winter areas fall is the best time to plant spring and summer-flowering perennials. Prepare soil thoroughly before planting, since perennials will remain in the same bed for several years. In sunny locations plant dianthus, gaillardia, hollyhock, lavender, penstemon, Shasta daisy, sweet William, verbena. In shady locations plant columbine, coral bells (Heuchera sanguinea), phlox, violets.

Chrysanthemums. Select new varieties from the flowering plants on display in nurseries. Continue to stake and tie long flowering stems. As the blooms fade, cut stems back to about 8 inches above the ground. Water plants in furrows or basins rather than overhead to prevent spread of disease and help keep plants from breaking. Watch for spider mites, thrips, and aphids and spray or dust with an all-purpose insecticide-fungicide when necessary.

Roses

They will reach peak fall bloom this month. Pick blossoms and remove faded flowers at least once a week to encourage more bloom. Keep plants well watered. Feed with complete fertilizer or a special rose food. This will be their last feeding until next spring. Container-grown roses available in nurseries can be set out now; be sure to select healthy, well formed plants.

Shrubs

This is one of the best months to plant container-grown shrubs. Dig planting holes at least two times the size of the root ball. Use a planting mix that contains recommended amounts of superphosphate and generous quantities of such organic materials as ground bark and peat moss. Keep well watered.

Azaleas, camellias, and gardenias. Some early flowering kinds of azaleas and camellias will start to bloom during November and December. Feed now with a fertilizer containing phosphorus and potash (but no nitrogen) to encourage bloom. If you didn't disbud camellias last month to encourage larger blooms, do so as soon as possible. To prevent damage to plants and developing buds, keep the soil around the roots of azaleas, camellias, and gardenias moist at all times, and protect plants from the hot sun and drying winds. Set out new selections of azaleas and camellias when temperatures cool. In areas where temperatures drop below freezing, wait until spring before you plant gardenias.

Mist-spray foliage in the early morning to help keep plants cool and to wash off dust.

Trees

Plant container-grown trees. Follow planting directions given for shrubs (above).

Citrus. As temperatures cool, trees need less moisture. Therefore, extend intervals between waterings, but never let plants wilt. To control scale insects, spray trees with an oil spray at summer dilution rates as soon as daytime temperatures are 75°.

Vegetables

Plant beets, broccoli, cabbage, carrots, cauliflower, chard, endive, kohlrabi, lettuce, onions, parsley, radishes, rutabagas, spinach, and turnips now. Be sure that winter sun reaches your vegetable garden. Prepare the soil carefully.

General Care

Fertilizing. Feed annuals and perennials set out last month with a complete plant food. This is the last month of the growing season to feed your hardy trees and shrubs with a complete plant food. Feed summer lawns with a fertilizer that is high in nitrogen.

Wait until after the second mowing before feeding annual rye and other newly planted lawns.

Grooming. Athough most heavy pruning of trees and shrubs is done during the winter months, you can improve their appearance by removing sucker growth and dead branches as well as shortening extra long growth now. Cover all cuts that are more than one inch in diameter with a pruning compound.

Remove sucker growth on trunks or from roots of trees such as paper mulberry (Broussonetia papyrifera), carob, olive, California pepper tree, and jujube (Ziziphus jujuba). Prune and shape hedges and espaliers.

Leaching. Flood several times around trees and shrubs and in flower beds and containers to wash out accumulations of harmful salts that have built up around roots during the summer months. Add a wetting agent to the water to increase its penetration.

Mulching. Spread ground bark, redwood chips, or other mulching material around the annuals and perennials that you set out this fall.

Watering. The winter lawns, annuals, perennials, bulbs, and container-grown plants that you planted this month will need careful watering. You may have to water new lawns and flower beds once a day to keep the soil moist. As the weather cools, intervals between waterings of established trees, shrubs, and summer lawns can be increased. When you do irrigate, be sure that moisture penetrates throughout the root zone. Syringe plants with a jet of water during the early morning hours to keep dust from accumulating on foliage.

Pest, Disease, and Weed Control

It's still important to syringe plants with a strong jet of water once or twice a week during the early morning hours to wash dust and many pests off of plants. When temperatures cool, aphids and mildew start to attack many plants. Control them with regular application of an all-purpose insecticide-fungicide. *Caution*: Do not spray plants with liquids when the sun is shining directly on plants and temperatures are above 85°. Continue applications of diazinon to control spider mites on junipers, pyracantha, and roses.

Chlorosis. As the weather cools during October and November, many trees and shrubs that showed signs of chlorosis during the hot summer will start active growth and turn green. If plants are slow to recover, leach harmful salts from the root area by flooding soil with water and a wetting agent. Mulch plants with

OCTOBER (continued)

peat moss, leaf mold, ground bark, or compost, and apply an iron chelate at recommended rates. Feed hardy plants with a complete fertilizer. Keep disease and insect pests under control; they weaken plants.

Weeds. Don't let weeds get ahead of you; it is much easier to remove the small ones than those whose roots are established. Spray with killers only when the air is still to prevent the material from drifting onto desirable plants. Follow all directions and precautions printed on the label.

November

Annuals

In mild-winter areas, you can still set out many annuals for winter and spring color. Unless plants set out earlier are already in the advanced bud stage, they probably won't bloom this winter in colder areas. Individual plants in bands suffer less setback and become established faster than transplants from flats. See October's entry for the kinds of annuals to plant.

Keep soil moist at all times and feed with a complete fertilizer at three or four-week intervals as soon as new growth starts. To encourage compact growth and more blooms, pinch tip growth of calendulas, nicotiana, petunias, snapdragons, stock, and sweet peas.

At elevations below 2,500 feet, continue to plant seedlings of such annuals as ageratum, African daisies, calendulas, candytuft, Iceland poppies, pansies, petunias, stock, and snapdragons.

Sweet peas. Plant seeds of the spring-flowering kinds or get seedlings in small pots from nurseries. Seeds germinate quickly when planted in warm soils this month. Dust seed with a fungicide to prevent disease. Plant them about an inch deep in a 12 to 18-inch-deep trench filled with good garden loam mixed with organic matter. Provide early support for the vigorous shoots. On very cold nights, protect young, tender plants of sweet peas by covering them with double sheets of newspaper fastened with clothespins onto the trellis or wire supports. Remove the paper in the morning so that the plants will get full sunlight during the day. In cold-winter areas, wait until spring before sowing seed.

Bulbs and Bulblike Plants

In mild-winter areas, plant anemones, crocus, daffodils, freesias, gladiolus, hyacinths, ranunculus, and tulips. You can plant low-growing annuals over the bulbs now to hide the fading foliage when the bulbs have finished blooming. (Tulip bulbs rarely live over a second year.) If you want to leave your daffodils in the ground for several years, set them 6 to 8 inches deep (depending on the size of bulbs). In low and middle elevation desert areas, plant daffodils in partial shade.

Cactus and Other Succulents

Move frost-tender kinds that are growing in containers to protected locations for the winter. Water less frequently and withhold fertilizer to increase the plants' resistance to frost.

Container Plants

To be sure the root ball is thoroughly soaked, water slowly until moisture seeps through the bottom. Do this at least every two weeks. If plants are rootbound, remove from container, and either prune roots and replant in the same container or shift to a larger one. Then soak soil with a dilute solution of transplanting hormone.

Lawns and Ground Covers

Lawns. This is the last month to plant a cool-season grass of Bermuda or hybrid Bermuda grass lawns. (In areas where temperatures are still warm, such as around Palm Springs, Yuma, and mild parts of the Salt River Valley, you can still overseed your summer lawn with a cool-season grass.)

Keep winter lawns moist, but not soaking wet. After planting, water the lawn frequently and lightly. As the grass becomes established, increase the amount of water applied and extend the intervals between irrigations. To prevent leggy growth, mow winter lawns at regular intervals. Cut rye and blue grass lawns to a height of 1½ inches, fescue grasses to 1½ to 2 inches. Don't mow or walk on the lawn when the soil is wet; you may compact the soil and damage the turf.

Ground covers. Late fall and winter are ideal times to set out such ground cover plants as dwarf coyote brush (*Baccharis pilularis*), prostrate pyracantha, ivy, rock cotoneaster (*C. horizontalis*), and creeping rosemary. If you plant them now, their roots become established during the cool winter months and plants are better able to survive the summer heat than those set out in spring.

Perennials

Plant winter and spring-flowering perennials to add color to borders or plantings of new shrubs and trees. Among the many kinds of perennials you can plant now up to an altitude of 5,000 feet are asters, carnations, columbine, coreopsis, dianthus (pinks), feverfew, gaillardia, penstemon, phlox, physostegia, red-hot poker, rudbeckia, Shasta daisies, statice (*Limonium*), sweet William, and violets.

Chrysanthemums. Late-flowering kinds are at their best now, and nurseries carry many varieties in full bloom ready to plant in your garden. Place stakes and ties around plants to prevent the bloom-heavy stems from sprawling on the ground. Remove faded blooms once or twice a week to keep plants neat and to encourage more flowers. As soon as plants have finished blooming, cut the stems back to within 8 inches of the ground.

Dahlias. When dahlia tops have died down, cut the tops to 6-inch stubs and lift the tubers carefully with a spading fork. Shake off loose soil, and store in a cool, frost-free place.

Roses

You can still set out container-grown roses. Plant them in a sunny location, in well drained soil high in organic matter such as ground bark, peat moss, or cottonseed hulls. Maintain a 2-inch-deep mulch around plants; keep roots moist, but not soaking wet, with regular deep irrigation. Withhold fertilizers until next spring. Bare-root plants will be available next month.

At the lower elevations of the Southwest desert, many kinds of roses are in full bloom. Remove faded blooms, rose hips, and sucker growth (vigorous shoots that appear from below the bud union). Keep roots moist with regular waterings until plants begin to become dormant.

Shrubs

Nurseries have a wide variety of excellent shrubs for planting this month. Next month, many bare-root shrubs will be available. Get planting areas ready now.

Azaleas and camellias. Each year desert nurseries offer gardeners a greater selection of the popular camellia shrubs. This is a good time to select some of the Japonica and Sasanqua varieties now beginning to bloom. Plant new selections in a well drained soil containing ample amounts of peat moss and finely ground bark. If your soil drains slowly, plant in raised beds or containers. Do not set plants any deeper than they were in the nursery flat or container.

Remove faded flowers on established plants so that new buds will have plenty of space to develop. Be careful not to break off the growth buds or new shoots next to the flower buds. Keep plants well watered.

Trees

Dig planting holes and prepare soil for the container-grown and bare-root trees that you intend to set out during the next few months. If you garden where caliche is a problem, you may want to read or re-read the section in the introduction for more information on planting in this type of soil.

If you wish to move a tree, prepare the planting hole well in advance and transplant during December or January when trees are in their most dormant stage. December is also a good time to plant frost-hardy trees from nursery containers. Trees need deep watering; apply water in large basins extending to the drip line of the tree.

Citrus. Water established trees that are growing in the ground about once a month during the winter. Water young trees or those growing in containers every week or two. Now is the time to start protecting citrus from frost injury.

Vegetables

As soon as they are available at nurseries, set out transplants of broccoli, cabbage, and cauliflower. You can also plant seeds of such cool-season vegetables as beets, carrots, leaf and head lettuce, onions, parsley, spinach, and turnips. For crisp, succulent vegetables, provide constant moisture, otherwise they'll become tough and fibrous.

General Care

Clean-up. Many deciduous trees, shrubs, and vines will turn color and shed their leaves this month. To keep your garden neat, rake this debris off lawns, patios, driveways, and paths. You may want to rent or buy a garden vacuum to make the job easier. Carefully remove leaves in flower and vegetable beds. Many desert gardeners use leaves from mesquite and palo verde trees as a mulch. You can grind up large leaves and twigs with a powder shredder, and use them to increase the organic matter content of your soil. Avoid using materials that may carry disease and insect pests on them.

Cultivate. Cultivate the soil around annuals, perennials, shrubs, trees, and vines, being careful not to injure roots (but do not cultivate around such shallow-rooted plants as azaleas, camellias, citrus, and hibiscus). Break the crust that forms at the soil surface to facilitate penetration of water and air into the soil. Regular cultivation controls weeds that rob the soil of moisture and nutrients.

Fertilize. Feed house plants with a fertilizer that is formulated for them. Apply fertilizer that contains phosphorus and potassium (but not nitrogen) to evergreen shrubs and trees.

To encourage vigorous growth, feed annuals set out last month with recommended rates of a complete plant food. After winter lawns have been mowed 2 or 3 times, apply a fertilizer that is high in nitrogen, such as ammonium sulfate

or ammonium phosphate.

Grooming. Shear hedges to keep them neat and compact. Also prune and thin out excess growth of hardy evergreen trees so that wind will pass through them easily. Don't prune roses, deciduous fruit and shade trees, and other deciduous plants until after they become dormant. Wait until spring before pruning frost-tender plants. The canopy of foliage serves to protect the inner portions of the plant from frost damage.

Mulching. Apply mulches of composted materials, ground bark, cottonseed hulls, peat moss, or leaf mold around plants.

Stake and tie plants. Be sure young trees are tied to strong stakes. It is also a good idea to stake newly planted camellias or other upright-growing shrubs to prevent them from being blown over by strong winds. Replace stakes that have rotted or have been outgrown by vigorous plants. Check all ties to be sure that they are tight enough to hold plants securely but don't cut into trunk or branches.

Watering. As the fall days get cooler, the garden will need less water. In areas where flood irrigation is practiced, winter schedules (approximately every 28 days) become effective this month. But don't let the soil dry out during the fall and winter months. Plants need moisture even during the coldest weather. In addition, damp soil retains warmth better than dry soil, thus lessening the chance of frost damage to plants growing in it. During cold weather, water in the morning so that the soil will warm up during the day.

Pest, Disease, and Weed Control

Powdery mildew, aphids, and thrips are among the most important disease and insect pests you'll have to contend with now. Spray or dust susceptible plants with an all-purpose insecticide to kill these insects and with a fungicide such as acti-dione (formulated to kill powdery mildew).

Weeds. Don't let them get ahead of you. Remove weeds from garden beds while they're still small and easy to pull. After you have thoroughly cultivated planting beds and added organic matter and fertilizer, water well 2 or 3 times before sowing seeds or setting out plants. If possible, cultivate between watering. This encourages weed seeds to germinate so that you can remove them easily before you plant in the bed.

Weather

Frost protection. Freezing temperatures strike many areas of the Southwest desert in November. As soon as possible, begin to protect all tender plants from frost damage. Even in mild-winter areas, Natal plum (*Carissa*), hibiscus, lantana, and poinsettia need frost protection.

December

Annuals

If you garden where winters are generally mild, as in the Salt River Valley or Tucson, Yuma, or Palm Springs areas, you can still plant many kinds of annuals from flats, bands, or small pots. Among them are African daisies, calendulas, cinerarias, lobelias, pansies, petunias, fairy primroses (*Primula malacoides*), snapdragons, stock, sweet alyssum, and violas.

To encourage bushy growth and more flowers, pinch back tip growth of calendulas, petunias, snapdragons, and sweet peas. Train sweet pea stems on wires or netting. Stake tall-growing plants such as snapdragons and stock. Feed annuals with a complete plant food about every three or four weeks. Keep annuals well mulched with ground bark, cottonseed hulls, peat moss, or leaf mold to help conserve moisture. Continue to remove or to cut back untidy plants.

Bamboo

Golden bamboo (*Phyllostachys aurea*), most commonly planted, thrives in many desert areas. During the winter months, leaves may take on a yellow look; usually this is a temporary condition. Leaves may burn in very cold winters, but new growth will emerge in spring. Since bamboo is a grass, it needs lots of water.

Bulbs and Bulblike Plants

Among the kinds you can plant now in mild-winter areas are: amaryllis, daylilies, gladiolus, hyacinths, lycoris, and tulips. To help prevent disease and insect pests from damaging them, do this before planting: Place about a pound of bulbs in a paper bag. Add a teaspoonful of a bulb dust and twist the top of the bag closed. Then shake the contents until all the bulbs have an even coating of the dust on them. Be sure to plant only firm, healthy bulbs; those that are soft may be diseased and should be discarded. Firm the soil around them so that there are no air pockets.

Lawns and Ground Covers

Lawns. Cool-season grasses, such as bluegrasses and annual rye, are growing vigorously now. Keep them in top shape by mowing and watering regularly. Also feed about once a month with a fertilizer high in nitrogen (ammonium sulfate). Water dichondra during early morning so it will be dry by evening; this helps prevent disease. Try to avoid walking on dichondra and lippia lawns when the leaves are covered with frost; the places where you walk will turn into dark patches, making the lawn unsightly. Dichondra lawns often turn yellowish during cold weather; when temperatures warm in the spring, the turf will become a rich green again. Wait until next spring to sow grass or dichondra lawns.

Ground covers. In mild-winter areas, take advantage of the cool weather to plant ground covers of dwarf rosemary, cerastium, coyote brush (*Baccharis pilularis*), blue festuca, and hardy ice plant (*Carpobrotus*). Although plants may not make much top growth during the winter months, roots will develop.

Perennials

December is a good time to plant or divide hardy asters, columbine, coreopsis, dianthus, feverfew, gaillardia, penstemon, Shasta daisies, sweet William, vinca, sweet violets. When dividing, discard weak plants. Unless you know the cause of the failure and expect to correct the problem, don't replant the same kind of perennial in a spot where it failed before. Plant in a good soil mix, and place mulch around plants to help retain moisture and to prevent frost damage to tender roots.

Chrysanthemums. Cut plants to the ground as soon as they have finished blooming. Discard weak and diseased plants, and clean up fallen leaves and debris from around the base of plants.

Roses

Roses are excellent gifts for your gardening friends. Prepare beds and planting holes for bare-root roses that will be available from nurseries this month.

In the low desert, wait until January 15 before pruning roses; at higher elevations wait until March 1. Too-early pruning may encourage tender growth during winter warm spells, resulting in a later damage by frosts. Plant bare-root roses as soon as they become available. You can plant container-grown roses at any time. If roses in your garden need transplanting, do it after they become dormant. For best results, buy plants with three or more sturdy canes (Number 1 grade) and grow them in a sunny position. Plant roses in a fast draining soil that contains generous amounts of peat moss, ground bark, or similar organic material. Set plants so the base of the bud union is about one inch above the soil surface.

Shrubs

Camellias. Shade blooming plants from the winter sun to protect flowers from sunburn during warm days. December and January are good months to transplant camellias, or to plant them into the garden from nursery containers. Give them a shady location and a well drained soil that contains at least 50 per cent organic matter. A north or east exposure with morning sun and afternoon shade is best.

Desert gardeners often plant camellias in raised beds or containers where plants can have a good soil and fast drainage. Planting in containers has the added advantage of making it possible to move camellias into protected areas during the hot summer months or in frosty periods in winter.

Protect plants from sudden drops in temperature as well as from wind. Plants growing in movable containers are most easily protected.

Trees

Plant bare-root deciduous shade and fruit trees as soon as possible after they become available in nurseries.

Citrus. Don't let plants wilt. During the winter, water citrus thoroughly, but only about half as often as you did during the summer. Many kinds of citrus fruit will ripen this month. Remove fruit that has fallen around the base of trees.

If you haven't provided frost protection for your citrus trees, do so as soon as possible. Do not plant citrus (adapted to mild-winter sections only) until after the danger of frost is past.

Vegetables

Keep your fall-planted vegetables watered. Earlier seeded crops such as lettuce may need protection on cold nights. Use plastic, bamboo screen, or other light material; remove covering in the daytime.

Vines

Grapes. Set out bare-root plants of grapes as soon as they become available in nurseries. Plant in full sun. Prepare holes at least 18 inches deep and wide. Set the bare-root plants so that all but the top 1 or 2 inches of the stem are below the surface of the ground. Water in thoroughly after planting.

General Care

Clean-up. Remove faded annuals, and cut back chrysanthemums and other perennials that have finished blooming. Remove dead or dying leaves of such plants as bananas, bird of paradise, elephant ears, palms. Prune out dead branches from trees and shrubs. Keep holiday decorations in mind when you prune out unwanted growth from pyracantha, cotoneaster, Burford holly, and strawberry tree.

Fertilizing. To keep winter lawns green and in active growth, feed with a high-nitrogen fertilizer at label-recommended rates at least once a month. If the annuals and perennials that you set out during October and November weren't fertilized at planting time, feed now with a complete fertilizer; otherwise, wait until February.

Grooming. Wait until the leaves of deciduous trees and shrubs have fallen before pruning them heavily; you can even put off this job until next month. Trees with dense crowns, such as African sumac (*Rhus lancea*), California pepper, elm, mulberry, olive, and Texas umbrella tree often break or blow over during heavy winds. To reduce wind resistance and chance breakage, thin excess branches now or in January. Shear hedges to keep them neat and compact. Delay pruning of tender plants until danger of frost is past.

When pruning deciduous shade trees, such as mulberry and elm, thin out branches. Don't trim them back in hair-cut fashion since this results in broom-like growth that destroys the natural shape of the trees. If it is necessary to lower the height of the tree, cut branches back to a lateral. Make clean cuts; don't leave stubs; paint cuts with pruning compound. Cut out dead palm fronds.

Watering. Even though many desert areas received generous amounts of rainfall during the fall, you still need to water your garden. However, intervals between watering can be longer than in the spring and summer months. Trees and large shrubs need deep soaking. Water fall-planted lawns and beds of annuals and vegetables as often as necessary to keep them moist. Before you water, check the soil with a probe or soil sampling tube to determine the need.

Planting

Soil preparation. Prepare soil in advance of planting roses, trees, and other kinds of plants, especially if you use steer manure. After incorporating manure with the soil, flood thoroughly to leach ammonia and salts from the manure. Although you can plant as soon as the mix is workable, some prefer to wait for several weeks.

Bare-root planting. This month, nurseries begin to receive shipments of bare-root trees, shrubs, and roses. For best choice, make your selections early.

Weather

Frost protection. Tender plants, such as bougainvillea, citrus, gardenia, hibiscus, lantana, and Natal plum, are damaged by the below-freezing temperatures that strike some parts of the Southwest desert. Tender plants (in all but the mildest desert areas) need protection during the next two or three months.

INDEX TO PLANTS

PHOTO CREDITS

William Aplin: pages 7, 12 (left), 14, 21 (bottom right), 25 (top, bottom right), 29, 30 (right), 31 (right), 32, 33 (right), 35, 36, 39, 40, 41, 42, 43, 45, 47 (bottom right), 48 (top), 49 (top, bottom right), 50, 54 (right), 55, 63 (bottom right), 68 (top right), 69 (top left, right), 73, 74 (top, bottom right), 75 (right), 78 (top right). **Ernest Braun:** pages 8, 17, 19 (top right), 25 (bottom left), 26 (bottom left), 27 (top left), 48 (bottom), 53 (top right). **Clyde Childress:** pages 15, 16. **Glenn M. Christiansen:** pages 9, 13 (left), 19 (top left), 20, 26 (top right), 33 (left), 44 (left), 46, 52, 54 (left), 56, 57, 58 (left), 59 (left), 61, 62, 63 (top), 64, 65, 66 (left), 67 (left), 72, 76, 77. **Robert C. Cleveland:** pages 12 (right), 49 (top left). **Richard Dawson:** pages 26 (top left), 34, 47 (top right), 58 (right), 70, 79 (bottom). **Donald Erskine:** page 31 (left). **Frank L. Gaynor:** pages 6, 19 (bottom right), 21 (top right), 23, 24. **Richard Jepperson:** pages 27 (bottom right), 69 (bottom). **Eric Johnson:** pages 27 (bottom left), 30 (left), 53 (top left), 74 (bottom right). **Markow Photography:** page 22. **Proctor Mellquist:** pages 13 (right), 59 (right), 60. **Virginia Moore:** page 51. **Don Normark:** pages 10, 18, 26 (bottom right), 37, 78 (top left). **Wm. M. Rowland:** page 47 (bottom left). **Salter Bros.:** page 11. **Bill Sears:** pages 28, 79 (top). **Darrow M. Watt:** pages 44 (right), 63 (left), 71. **Joe Williamson:** 66 (right), 67 (right), 68 (top left).